Singular
Voices

Other Poetry Anthologies
from Avon Books:

AMERICAN POETRY ANTHOLOGY,
Daniel Halpern, Ed.
NEW YORK: POEMS, *Howard Moss, Ed.*
VOICES WITHIN THE ARK, *Howard Schwartz &
Anthony Rudolf, Eds.*

Singular Voices

AMERICAN POETRY TODAY

Edited by
STEPHEN BERG

 AVON
PUBLISHERS OF BARD, CAMELOT, DISCUS AND FLARE BOOKS

SINGULAR VOICES: AMERICAN POETRY TODAY is
an original publication of Avon Books. This work has
never before appeared in book form.

AVON BOOKS
A division of
The Hearst Corporation
1790 Broadway
New York, New York 10019

Copyright © 1985 by Stephen Berg
Published by arrangement with American Poetry Review
Library of Congress Catalog Card Number: 84-45585
ISBN: 0-380-89876-4

Library of Congress Cataloging in Publication Data
Main entry under title:

Singular voices.

    1. American poetry—20th century.   I. Berg, Stephen.
PS615.S48 1985   811'.52'08   84-45585
ISBN 0-380-89876-4

First Avon Printing, March 1985

OPB   10 9 8 7 6 5 4 3 2 1

For Richard Hugo

GREEN STONE

All stones have luck built in. Some
a lucky line that curves a weak green back
into some age prehuman. If stones
could talk they'd tell us how they've survived.
They've been used in beautiful fences,
been weapons hurled.

The luck of a stone is part of that stone.
It's not mystical, does not exist just on
the stone like a spell put there by some spirit
in some awkward moment—say the picnic's
on the verge of disaster, then good wine opened
and the sun suddenly out, and oh the laughter.
But why am I digressing?
These things have nothing to do with stone luck.

I'm speaking real stones. You understand.
Rocks. Not symbols for testicles and not
some lay philosopher's metaphysical notion
of an indestructible truth. Real stones, the ones
you find lining ocean floors or creek beds
or lying lonely on roads. Probable colors:
blue, yellow, gray, red, green, white or brown.
The luck of each is the same but each suited
to a different situation. That's why December,
told I was dying of cancer
I picked up a green stone I liked the look of
and carried it in my pocket.

I fondled it just before I took the plane to Seattle.
I kissed it often, both sides before the plane took off,
before biopsy, before major surgery. And now
that surgery seems to have gotten every flake
of sick tissue, I keep the stone on a ledge,
where every morning the sun warms the stone.
When I'm totally recovered, another three months
they say, I'll throw the stone back where I found it.
I won't tell you where that is.
The same rock would not work for you no matter
how trivial your problem, how little
luck you need. Please know
I want your life to go on same as mine.
It's just essential you find your own stone.
It lies somewhere near you now, innocent,
and your eye will spot it in one right moment.
You must hold it close to your ear, and
when it speaks to you, you must respond.

—Richard Hugo

INTRODUCTION

I conceived this book for a few simple reasons. First, I wanted to bring together poems by living American poets whose work exemplifies strong new styles. There may be few today of Yeats's, Williams's, or Stevens's stature, but that doesn't matter. What we have is a wealth of original voices: some leaning on structures of prose fiction; some involved in the uses of traditional prosodic forms; some eclectic, wandering among the endless formal possibilities of a territory between poetry and prose. Each poet in this book writes his or her own kind of poem, yet it would be hard to predict what kind of poem any of them will write next.

Respect for the power of narrative, for content drawn from the ordinary world one lives in, seems to dominate much of the new poetry, but ideas nakedly stated also shape the poetry of our time. An obsession with prose clarity, a moral drive toward significance immediately and clearly revealed, informs the complex passions of these poems: a desire to speak sincerely of what one feels and knows, not without freedom of imagination but also not without a commitment to discover durable meaning in a time of lost standards, when millions of human lives can be bulldozed and tortured out of existence, and when few seem able to say what "good" poetry is. I think Milosz's words express the basic underlying esthetic and ethical restlessness of these poems: "Each of us is so ashamed of his own helplessness and ignorance that he considers it appropriate to communicate only what he thinks others will understand. There are, however, times when somehow we slowly divest ourselves of that shame and begin to speak openly about all the things we do not understand.'' Perhaps, then, we have a new poetry of conscience, a poetry that aims to change who we are and what we do with each other and with nature.

I decided to include only one poem per poet because I wanted to make room for the other main part of my conception—a belief that the poet, in writing about his or her own poem, would write the most helpful ''criticism'' for literate readers. ''Go ask the poets,'' Freud said in another context, and his advice applies here equally well. The reader won't find attempts to establish theories into which all poetry must fit; there are no flashing career swords, no need to rank or compare. Faced with their own poems, in fact, the poets were driven to talk about the difficulties of creation and interpretation and just plain understanding, and to come up with fresh, personal ways to guide the reader. It is difficult, therefore, to separate writer from reader: each wants to explain to himself what has happened between him and the poem—a lucky problem. In these essays you can taste the confusion and honest ignorance and discovery appropriate to the innocence behind *any* good reader's approach to a text.

But above all, the variety of thematic passion shared in eloquent voices makes these poems live. James Dickey's utterances of love to a young woman; Bell's weird quest in an Italian hotel room; Forché's character Anna and her private political history in ''Endurance''; Gallagher's ''When a taboo is broken there is often the feeling of freshness . . .''; Glück's explanation of love and our lust for oblivion; Graham's poem on Klimt's painting, which leads her back to Buchenwald; Hall's mysterious sheep; Kinnell's analytic anger at Hiroshima and Nagasaki as they continue to echo their sad detail; Kunitz's myth of rapture and dread; Levertov's lament, a nature poem against nuclear war; Milosz's elegy, tender, political, to an old love; Plumly's resurrection of Keats near death; Ryan's Henry James dream that leads him back to a loving memory of his mother; Snodgrass's intricate musical portrait of apple trees; Stern's pitiable mosquitoes transformed into Mexican workers; Weiss's lost, longed-for Hungarian father; Williams's searing depiction of Vietnam vets, ending at night with one in his wheelchair plowing a figure eight in the snow. These sketches of some of what will be found in the poems say almost nothing about the equally dramatic discussions of the poems—their intimacy of response, their unexpected revelations: a missing detail supplied, a dark line explained and clarified, a source dug up, an attitude toward life rejected, revised—technical matters, political matters, private matters, ways of seeing everyday events. The struggle and grace in these poems and essays you may well recognize as your own on any given day as you try to understand your life.

What I believe *Singular Voices* offers is an unpredictable cache of poems and essays durable enough to enter the reader's life, stay there, and affect it. That means they will feel necessary to us: moving versions of our personal/historical experience. These poems and essays are also a substantial introduction to what is happening in American poetry today, and to how and what those who write poems think about it— talking to themselves, to friends, to students in a class, to any dedicated reader. In the essays, I hoped the personal, literary, and political would fuse as they do in many of the poems, and in life. I hoped the writers would avoid the arrogant esotericism of some critics, who do not write poetry, and instead articulate an awareness of contradictory responses to particular poems and to the changing nature of poetry. No editor can predict the outcome of his wishes, but I can now say that as a reader among readers I am grateful for the results: pleasure, instruction, sincerity, the warmth of so many crucial, humane presences.

—Stephen Berg
1983

EDITOR'S NOTE

By nature such collections are limited: money, space, circumstance. Some poets were unable to deliver, or declined. Taste also keeps this from being comprehensively representative instead of a wide personal selection. Another editor would no doubt have produced a very different book. Snyder, Ginsberg, Creeley, Oppen, Duncan, Ashbery, Valentine, Logan, Gibbins, Dugan, Lieberman, Hecht, are only some of the poets whose work I wish could have been included.

Opportunities emerged in the course of putting *Singular Voices* together. When Galway Kinnell informed me that his hectic schedule would prevent him from writing an essay, I asked Ted Solotaroff if he would be the one nonpoet critic in the book and write about Galway's poem. Fortunately, he agreed. John Ashbery declined, on principle, to have a poem of his included in a book of this kind (poets writing about their own work), but he plans to write an essay arguing against the main assumption of the book, and I hope we will see it soon.

CONTENTS

xv

ACKNOWLEDGMENTS

MARVIN BELL: "A True Story" from *Drawn by Stones, by Earth, by Things that Have Been in the Fire*, published by Atheneum Publishers, 1984.

ROBERT BLY: "August Rain" © by Robert Bly. Printed by permission of the author.

HAYDEN CARRUTH: "The Cows at Night," from *From Snow and Rock, From Chaos*, copyright © 1968 by Hayden Carruth, originally appeared in *Poetry* in 1968 and is reprinted by permission of New Directions Publishing Corporation.

JAMES DICKEY: "Deborah as Scion" (I & II), from *Puella*, copright © 1982 by James Dickey, is reprinted by permission of the author. It originally appeared in *Poetry*, and *Puella*, Doubleday and Co., Inc., 1982.

STEPHEN DOBYNS: "Cemetery Nights," copyright © by Stephen Dobyns 1984, is reprinted by permission of the author.

CAROLYN FORCHÉ: "Endurance," from *The Country Between Us*, copyright © 1981 by Carolyn Forché, is reprinted by permission of Harper and Row Publishers, Inc.

TESS GALLAGHER: "Each Bird Walking," from *Willingly*, copyright © 1984 by Tess Gallagher, published by Gray Wolf Press, is reprinted by permission of the author.

LOUISE GLÜCK: "Night Song," copyright © 1985 by Louise Glück, is printed by permission of the author.

JORIE GRAHAM: "Two Paintings by Gustav Klimt," from *Hybrids of Plants and Ghosts*, Princeton University Press, 1981, originally appeared in *The American Poetry Review*, Vol. 10/No. 3, and is reprinted by permission of the author.

DONALD HALL: "The Black Faced Sheep," from *Kicking the Leaves*, copyright © 1976 by Donald Hall, is reprinted by permission of Harper and Row Publishers, Inc., and the author.

ROBERT HASS: "The Harbor at Seattle," copyright © 1985 by Robert Hass, is printed by permission of the author.

DONALD JUSTICE: "On the Porch" and "At the Cemetery," copyright © 1982 by Donald Justice, originally appeared in *The Atlantic Monthly*. Thanks for permission to reprint. "On the Farm," copyright © 1983 by Donald Justice, originally appeared in *Ploughshares*. Thanks for permission to reprint. "On the Train," copyright © by Donald Justice, originally appeared in the *New Yorker* magazine. Thanks for permission to reprint.

GALWAY KINNELL: "The Fundamental Project of Technology," copyright © 1984 by Galway Kinnell, originally appeared in *The American Poetry Review*, Vol. 13/No. 4, July/August 1984. Thanks for permission to reprint.

ETHERIDGE KNIGHT: "The Idea of Ancestry," from *Poems from Prison* and *Belly Song*, copyright © 1968, 1973 by Etheridge Knight, is reprinted by permission of Broadside Press and the author.

GERALD STERN: "Baja," from *Paradise Poems*, Random House Publishers, © by Gerald Stern. Reprinted by permission of the author.

LUCIEN STRYK: "Awakening," © by Lucien Stryk and Swallow/Ohio University Press. Reprinted by permission of the author.

ROBERT PENN WARREN: "Recollection Long Ago: Sad Music," copyright © by Robert Penn Warren, is printed by permission of the author.

THEODORE WEISS: "The Death of Fathers," from *A Slow Fuse*, copyright © 1984 by Theodore Weiss, published by Macmillan Publishing Company, is reprinted by permission of the author.

RICHARD WILBUR: "Lying," copryight © 1983 by Richard Wilbur, originally appeared in the *New Yorker* magazine. Thanks for permission to reprint.

C.K. WILLIAMS: "From my Window," from *Tar*, copyright © 1983 by C.K. Williams, originally appeared in *The Paris Review* and is reprinted by permission of the author.

My thanks to Bob Wyatt for his faith in this book, and to John Douglas for helping me to finish it.

MARVIN BELL

A True Story

One afternoon in my room
in Rome,
I found, wedged
next to the wheel of a wardrobe,
so far under
no maid's broom could touch it,
a pouch made from a sock.
Inside were diamonds
in several sizes. Spread on the carpet,
they caught in my throat.
I knew that, from that moment on,
I would never answer the door.
All of my holiday
would be a preparation
for leaving. First,
I would have to leave the hotel,
probably the city.
I knew someone I could trust
and another with nerve.
She would carry home
half of them, perhaps in her underwear,
if it was not of the kind
customs officers like to touch.
I would carry the others
by way of Zurich,
stopping to purchase
eucalyptus cigarettes, chocolates
and a modest music box
with its insides exposed.
After that, who knows?
Keep them for years?
Lug them into the shade and sell cheap?

A trip to a third country?
A middleman?
So long as I didn't look up,
there with the stones before me
in the old room in the old city—
where embellishment of every fixture
and centuries of detail
took precedence
over every consideration
of light, air or space—
so long as I did not look up
to my suspicion,
I held the endless light of a fortune
and the course of a lifetime.

In retrospect, it was entirely appropriate
that my diamonds
were the ordinary pieces
of a chandelier, one string of which
had been pulled down
by a previous tenant of room three,
perhaps in a fit of ecstasy.
For I found, also—a diamond-
shaped third of its cover
hanging down from behind the wardrobe,
face to the wall—
the current issue of one of those men's
monthlies in which half-
nude women, glossy with wealth,
ooze to escape
from their lingerie.
And in the single page in its center,
someone had held his favorite
long enough to make love.
The pages were stuck together elsewhere also,
in no pattern,
and the articles on clothing and manners
left untouched.

* * *

So this was no ordinary hotel room,
or the most ordinary of all!
Men had come here many times no doubt
to make love by themselves.
But now
it was also a place of hidden treasure.
The rush of wealth and dark promise
I took from that room
I also put back. And so too everyone
who, when in Rome,
will do what the Romans do.

In the Heaven of the Diamond, I Would Flower Again: Overtaking "A True Story"

1

"A True Story" is a true story. Like the articles in the magazine, *True Story*, it is partly confession. It smacks of crime, sex, and secrecy. Is it a poem at all?

I had gone to Rome to see Venice, in part because I had grown up where the Great South Bay, Long Island Sound, and Atlantic Ocean meet, off the south shore of eastern Long Island. Please, my part of Long Island has little in common with New York City or the bedroom towns that extend eastward from it. Nor does it share much with those villages farther out on the Island where commuters from the City make up weekends and summers.

When I was born (August 3, 1937), we lived on the "wrong side" of the Long Island Railroad tracks, Whites among the Blacks, in Center Moriches. Center Moriches held maybe twenty-five hundred residents then and holds perhaps three thousand now. It does not swell up in the summer, though it can try one's patience to cross Main Street on a Sunday when city people are bumper to bumper headlong to the beaches.

Every street going south ends at the Bay, and many of those that go east and west lead to inlets or canals. There are more docks than beaches in Center Moriches. These docks—the largest of them known as Brooklyn Dock, others named according to the streets that lead to them: Inwood, Red Bridge Road, etc.—don't look like yachting harbors in Monterey. Rotting wood, car tires for bumpers, places from which to fish with a pin for a minnow or a ring of meat for crabs. One canal comes almost to the center of town. "Uncle John" kept his muddy clammer there. Nearby, down a path through weeds, was our idea of a shipyard, where small boats were built,

7

caulked, and stored. As kids, we snuck into the doctor's boat-house to loiter in his fancy cruiser, and sometimes "bor-rowed" a rough-hewn boat from the canal for the day. As for beaches, that was for Westhampton, which played to tourists, and Fire Island, which couldn't help it. Fishermen aren't swimmers. To them, the sea is a farm. Also, the belief lingers that, if one falls into the cold Atlantic, it is just easier not to try to swim. There were occasional drownings in the news and, on those uncommon occasions when the family wanted to "spend a day at the beach," we would drive away from Center Moriches for more than an hour.

Potato farms and duck farms. Volunteer firemen. Soccer in-stead of football. Leather jackets, switchblades, lots of fight-ing but no gangs. Mixed in among the WASPs were mostly Poles and Italians, with a smattering of others, such as my father, an immigrant from the Ukraine. The special outing of a year was a supper-club, theater, or ball-game trip to New York City. Of course, one always came home at night. The dream of a lifetime was a trip to California, but most people settled for Miami Beach. No one went to Harvard, and few would go to a college of any kind.

Growing up among people for whom English was a second language (if not for them, certainly for their parents), among people who lived in a seaside developer's dream and thought only of individual labor, among people who had survived harsh governments and difficult times, and to whom verbal skill was a sign of intelligence and carried a responsibility to a bedrock of reality—coming from that place and those people, I bear the small-town worker's attitude toward the notion that one can tell a lie to reveal the truth. That is, I don't believe it. I believe that the poet must bear witness honestly, lest he de-prive poetry of its authority and doom it to the role of light en-tertainment.

Hemingway said that a writer needed a "built-in, shock-proof shit detector." I like to think that I possess a first-rate bullshit meter, which I owe to the sort of people who never thought to try to sell the scenery.

2

I was crawling around the mud-colored rug in my room in Rome looking for some small thing I had dropped.

What was I looking for in Rome, on my way to Venice? Believe it or not (this is a true story, after all), I thought I knew. I knew that I hadn't gone as far as I was going. Italy was not my destination, nor even Venice. They were to be stopovers to a further place in my head—actually, in my heart.

Hence, I had written something about that upcoming visit to Italy before going! Titled "Italian," it discusses what "Marvin, on his first scared journey / to Italy . . . must be looking for. . . . A sky to go home in? . . . God, / how he hopes he hasn't come / just for a self-portrait."

There are some possibilities in the language: "He wants to know which word means really. / He wants to know which word tells where two streets meet, / which word means turning around fast. He wants to know which word means not tied. / And which means frightening." In the end, it's an image from the watery landscape of the poet's childhood, that place left behind, which he attaches, by will and wonder, to the place out ahead of him: "Once he put a hand / into the water somewhere in a flat wintry light / and the whitefish were the bones of diamonds, / so why not anyone?"

It's the lingering truth of—what?—fifth grade? The bones of men and women, and of all other animals, become coal in the earth and then diamonds. Even in grade school, the geologic notion of a "life beyond this life" had been more convincing to me than any religious metaphor. In the heaven of the diamond, I would flower again. James Wright, one of the great visionary, humane poets of my time, who himself went to Italy in his maturity to find the people, *his* people ("why not anyone?"), *himself* ("why not anyone?"), had made the same forecast in certain poems, of which the best known may be "The Jewel," with its famous ending: "When I stand upright in the wind, / My bones turn to dark emeralds."

At the far end of the journey which began for me with the poem "Italian" would be another new poem, "Florence," —in fact set in Florence, Rome, and Venice all at once. In it, the poet endures "the same craziness from not being able to speak / that made Kandinsky Kandinsky, / and makes the babbling pigeon lady of San Marco Square / talk to a mop." In the end, he goes into hiding "among you." Obviously, he is still on his way to that place in his heart which he hopes to know in his mind when he arrives.

In between the forecasting of "Italian," written before going, and the accommodations of "Florence," composed just afterward, comes the event at the center of "A True Story." Yet "A True Story" was not written until some months after coming home.

3

The plot of my poem is set down precisely as it happened. Surely I had stumbled onto treasure. After all, a pouch made from a sock? And clearly well hidden! Too heavy to be drugs. Too lumpy to be coins.

I was ready to find diamonds. Among all that stone—fountains, facades, statuary—I was prepared to discover a personal fortune. Among all that stationary culture and the long onslaught of barbarous history, I was set to come upon negotiable riches. After all, I was in Rome!, housed in the old Hotel Portoghesi, which sits in a tangle of perfectly crooked streets in the Old City, and faces, across the narrow Via dei Portoghesi, the bulbous facade of an ancient and windowless tower.

Such fortunes are not for you and me—not for me, anyway. My delusion of riches remained just long enough for me to begin to ponder how I might manage to keep them. For they would be a dangerous burden.

That fanciful burden, that once-in-a-lifetime chance, that One Big Score, soon lifted off from my shoulders and left me with the inescapable reality. Someone had broken the chandelier and, out of embarrassment and guilt, had hidden the pieces in a sock. I continue to wonder why he had not simply taken the pieces with him to discard in the street. And why had he gone to the trouble to fashion a pouch from a sock?

Wouldn't the whole sock have served as well as this one, severed high on the ankle? A thick, brown half-sock.

Of course, more than diamonds had been left for me. Was he that ashamed, that he had had to hide behind the wardrobe his soiled copy of *Playboy*? How intimate that room had become! Hadn't he exposed himself there, for me? Hadn't he left behind the clues, the permission and the unending need? Wasn't he a human being like myself? His fingerprints and his dried semen were, like it or not, what I had come to Rome to find. But not possess. For there can be no possession in this universe of discrete bodies. Then what is one to do with what it is one comes to know? Put it back where one found it, perhaps. Yes, put it back. Let the treasure remain for others to discover. For discovery is the cutting edge, the *diamond*, of experience, and experience is more than mere knowledge. Knowing, one might recommend the very hotel, and the room.

When "A True Story" is read aloud at public gatherings, the sentence with which it ends elicits both groans and gasps. No doubt, some are votes for a different ending. The poem, simply put, refuses to be cryptic. Instead, it is bald, audacious and impure: bald in plot, audacious in its mixture of the objects of our desire, and aesthetically "impure" in its insistence that it matters for us to know what is true. Let us consider the notions of discretion and indiscretion, and the designations "pure" and "impure"—as well as diamonds stained by desire.

"A True Story" is a true story. I recognize that because it is open-faced, skeletal and, some might say, vulgar, it intentionally fails many common literary expectations. I recognize also that, like a man exposed in his absence, it gives us, as if by accident, one more chance to forego judgment.

ROBERT BLY

August Rain

After a month and a half without rain, at last, in late August, darkness comes at three in the afternoon. A cheerful thunder begins, and then the rain. I set a glass out on a table to measure the rain, and, suddenly buoyant and affectionate, go indoors to find my children. They are upstairs, playing quietly alone in their doll-filled rooms, hanging pictures, thoughtfully moving "the small things that make them happy" from one side of the room to another. I feel triumphant, without need of money, far from the grave. I walk over the grass, watching the soaked chairs, and the cooled towels, and sit down on my stoop, pulling a chair out with me. The rain deepens. It rolls off the porch roof, making a great puddle near me. The bubbles slide toward the puddle edge, become crowded, and disappear. The black earth turns blacker; it absorbs the rain needles without a sound. The sky is low, everything silent, as when parents are angry . . . What has failed and been forgiven—the leaves from last year unable to go on, lying near the foundation, dry under the porch, retreat farther into the shadow, they give off a faint hum, as of birds' eggs, or the tail of a dog.

The older we get the more we fail, but the more we fail the more we feel a part of the dead straw of the universe, the corner of a barn with cow dung twenty years old, the chair fallen back on its head in a deserted farmhouse, the belt left hanging over the chairback after the bachelor has died in the ambulance on the way to the city. These objects belong to us; they ride us as the child holds on to the dog's fur; they appear in our dreams; they approach nearer and nearer, coming in slowly from the wainscoting. They make our trunks heavy, accumulating between trips. These objects lie against the ship's side, and will nudge the hole open that lets the water in at last.

15

The Mind Playing

I write prose poems when I long for intimacy. I want it from my friends, and I want it in poetry. Poems that speak with an intimate voice are often struggling against self-love—I feel that quiet voice in Baudelaire's prose poems—and we too long for the state of mind or soul when we let other things be. Allowing ourselves to become attentive to an object, we often become attentive to the reader as well. In that state of mind or state of soul we do not consciously or unconsciously plan to instruct other people.

I find myself concentrating on an object when I write prose poems, so I call this sort of prose poem a "thing poem." Its nearest relative is not the essay or the short story but the haiku, which evolved in Buddhist Japan through the determination of Buddhist poets to share the universe with flies, bears, and moonlight, and not declare which is more "sentient." The good haiku poem endures as evidence that the Buddhist poet has overcome, at least for this moment, the category mind that makes mutually exclusive inner and outer, human and animal, reason and instinct. Issa, a Pure Land Buddhist, died lying in a corncrib during a light snow. His death poem went this way:

This snow on the bedquilt—
this too
is from the Pure Land.

One sort of prose poem comes from the long tradition of the fable; another from the tradition of colorful and spectacular writing, as in Rimbaud's *Illuminations*; the prose poems I write belong to the tradition of Jiménez and Francis Ponge, and pays respect to their love of minute particulars. Ponge says:

In these terms, one will surely understand what I con-
sider to be the function of poetry. It is to nourish the spirit
of man by giving him the cosmos to suckle. We have only
to lower our standard of dominating nature and to raise
our standard of participating in it in order to make the
reconciliation take place. (Translation by Beth Archer)

The masters of the genre—Jiménez, Ponge, Tranströmer,
James Wright—share this aim.

When I write a thing poem, I think of it as a genre (it is not
private to me), but not as a form (it is so private one cannot tell
anyone else how to do it). Form agrees to a tension between
private spontaneity and the hard impersonal. The snail gives
his private substance to his private skin or shell, but its curve
is utterly impersonal, and follows the Fibonacci sequence.
Form in art and poetry follows this model.

No one can mistake the impersonal side of the sonnet: the
impersonal includes fourteen lines of ten syllables each, for a
total of one hundred forty syllables; two or sometimes four
thought units, apportioned among three quatrains and a
couplet; fourteen rhymed lines, and a beat system based on
relative loudnesses or stresses, calling for alternating loud-
nesses beginning with a soft tone.

The impersonal side of the haiku amounts to seventeen syl-
lables, a clear indication of which season the poem takes place
in, and interlocking sounds. Each great haiku holds inside it a
tiny explosion that indicates that some category, or arrogance,
or habit is being set aside, but that belongs more to the soft or
personal side.

The prose poem has no such great tension; it reaches to-
ward no such impersonal shell, or no such hard agreement
with the ancestors. It seems to experience little tension be-
tween what wants to be and what we've agreed has to be.

One indication that the prose poem is not yet a form is that
it is so difficult to finish one. Rewriting goes on for years. A
poem in form when done seems like an oak tree—finished.

And yet I love to write prose poems, and if someone says
they are not poetry at all, but prose, I won't contradict him. If
someone says it is not a form, I say it is a partially evolved

form, not yet able to reproduce itself. The thing poem encourages a kind of density in language, as in "August Rain," that delights me. Sometimes a single wolverine's claw pleases us with its character density. Sometimes a fox and a human being play together best when no loud sounds are heard. When relaxed and aware of no patterns, the mind sometimes gracefully allows itself to play with something equally graceful in nature, and the human being does not make the bit of nature feel small by insisting that his piece is art, even though he knows it is.

HAYDEN CARRUTH

The Cows at Night

The moon was like a full cup tonight,
too heavy, and sank in the mist
soon after dark, leaving for light

faint stars and the silver leaves
of milkweed beside the road,
gleaming before my car.

Yet I like driving at night
in summer and in Vermont:
the brown road through the mist

of mountain-dark, among farms
so quiet, and the roadside willows
opening out where I saw

the cows. Always a shock
to remember them there, those
great breathings close in the dark.

I stopped. I took my flashlight
to the pasture fence. They turned
to me where they lay, sad

and beautiful faces in the dark,
and I counted them—forty
near and far in the pasture,

turning to me, sad and beautiful
like girls very long ago
who were innocent, and sad

because they were innocent,
and beautiful because they were
sad. I switched off my light.

But I did not want to go,
not yet, nor knew what to do
if I should stay, for how

in that great darkness could I explain
anything, anything at all.
I stood by the fence. And then

very gently it began to rain.

God Sniffed and Said

"At all events, Adam, the time has come for you to start naming, whether you like it or not." And He looked somewhat frowningly around Him.

"I don't like it," Adam said.

"Evidently not. But why?"

"It wasn't part of the bargain."

"Bargain? What bargain? There wasn't any bargain."

"Implicitly in the act of creation You—"

"Nonsense," God interrupted. "What is this *implicitly*?"

"It means—"

God interrupted again. "What is this *means*?"

"I'm trying to tell You if You'd only let me."

"Tell Me? What can you tell Me that I don't already know. Knowing is my business."

Adam took a deep breath. "Then why don't You know that when You create somebody You become responsible for him and You're supposed to do the dirty work?"

"Responsible? I absolutely disacknowledge any such principle in My Absoluteness. Besides, I thought naming would be fun."

"Maybe," Adam said. "It does have a kind of exciting promise. Yet at the same time it fills me with strange foreboding. Something tells me that—"

"Foreboding? That's not supposed to come until later. After all, I only created you a few minutes ago."

"Oh? Funny, I feel as if I'd been here a long time already."

"Only in My mind," God said.

"Yes, that's just it—in Your mind. And if I'm supposed to do the naming, then the naming must exist in Your mind too. Why don't You go ahead and do it?"

"You don't understand."

"That's a fact," Adam said. Then: "Who the hell am I anyway? Do You know?"

"I know everything."

"Then what's this all about? And why won't You tell me?"

God sniffed again. "This is getting too complicated. Let's start over."

"OK," Adam said. "What do I do?"

"Take a look around."

"At what? You mean all these . . . these *things*?"

"There. You see? You've already started."

"You mean *things*?"

"Obviously. A fine name. Fundamental, in fact."

"You mean these . . . these *objects*?"

"Aha! Already beginning to perceive abstractly."

"These . . . *subjects*?"

"Wow! A real leap. You're doing splendidly."

All at once Adam began rattling off names. "*Spinach. Crustacean. Helicopter. Bargain basement. Dinosaur. Asia Minor. Mincemeat. Thorn. The Sleeping Beauty. Heliotrope. Pork chop. Bread-and-butter pickles. Muskrat Ramble. Polar bear. Cadillac. Grandson. Vibration. Macaroni. The Monroe Doctrine. Dodecaphonalism. Rattlesnake. Clan. Cypress. Missing link. . . .*"

"Wonderful!" God said. "You got the range now."

"*Ox. Yoke. Wagon. Wagon wheel. Squeak. Grease. Petroleum. Rockefeller. Exxon. Imperialism. Starvation.* I could go on forever."

"Marvelous! Superb!" God beamed.

"Yeah, maybe," Adam said. "But I still don't quite like it."

"Why not?"

"Because every time I say a name, something comes busting out at me, shining all over with . . . with *reality*. Hey, how's that for a name?"

"Fine. Fine. But let's not get carried away."

"That's just what I mean. I am getting carried away. That's what gives me the foreboding. Don't You see? I thought this was Your job."

"Well, I did My job, didn't I? I'm the One who created all these . . . these . . ."

"*Things*?" Adam said.

"I guess so."

"But *things* is my invention. Do You mean You created all this mess without any reality? That's ridiculous."

"Now then. Don't be presumptuous."

"Presumptuous! If Somebody around here is presuming, I guess we know Who."

God sniffed. "Maybe. Maybe not."

"Holy cow," Adam said. "Don't pull that Godliness on me."

"Cow? What holy cow?"

"Why, that one over there. That cow."

"I don't see anything holy about that. It doesn't even look like *cow* to Me."

"Of course it's *cow*."

"Why?"

"Because I said so. Why else? Look, You're the one that got me started on this."

"OK. Calm yourself. But why is that a cow?"

"Because . . . because . . . Damn it, she's a cow, that's all. She's—"

"*She*? *She* doesn't exist yet. That's the next thing on the program."

"Don't be silly. I've known *she* as far back as I can remember, which is getting to be more or less like a million years."

"Hmmm."

"How can you have *things* without *she*?" Adam paused. "Still, if she isn't created yet, maybe that's what gives me this sense of foreboding."

"Why?"

"Well, I have this feeling somebody is going to screw her up."

"Who?"

"Don't ask."

"This is getting us nowhere," God said. "Let's go back to the cow."

"A damn fine cow, if you ask me."

"I'm not sure I did. But what's so special about it? Looks like an ordinary cow to me."

"It? Ordinary? She's a *she*. And if she's a cow, she has to be a fine one."

"How come?"

"Because . . . well, because she's Hathor, she's Devi, she's—"

"Names. Names."

"You bet. She's Ishtar, she's Aphrodite, she's covered all over with a golden aura." Adam squinted dreamily. "Why, a hell of a long, long way down the line I can even dimly see a poem called 'The Cows at Night.' "

"*Poem*? What's that?"

"You wouldn't know."

"Another one of your names, I suppose."

"So what? I did my job, didn't I? I did what You told me. I named everything."

"I reckon you did at that."

"All except one," Adam said.

"Which one?"

"Me! Me! *Adam*! You're the Namer who invented that name. Now I've been telling You what everything means, why don't You tell me what that means? Damn it, I've got a right to know."

"So you say."

"And what about the name *God*? Who invented that?"

God gave His Final Sniff. The discussion ended.

JAMES DICKEY

Deborah as Scion

I

With Rose, at Cemetery

Kin: quiet grasses.   Above,
Lace: white logic   fretted cloud-cloth.
                    In steady-state insolence
                I bring up a family
Look: a look like sword-grass, that will leave on anything human
    A swirl-cut, the unfurling touch of a world-wound
                Given straight out
    Of my forehead, and having all the work and tide-
pull of the dead, from their oblong, thrilling frame-tension
            Filled here with sunlight.

                God give me them,
        God gave them me, with a hedgerow grip on a rose
And black brows: in over-sifted, high-concentrate cloth
        And a high-fashion nudity, that shall come
    Of it, when the time comes.
                        Now at any good time
    Of this struck eleven o'clock, I can look forth on you
        Or anyone, as though you were being grazed
            Forever by a final tense of threads,
        The inmost brimming feather-hone of light.

            The dead work into a rose
            By back-breaking leisure, head-up
            Grave-dirt exploding like powder
    Into sunlit lace, and I lie and look back through their labor
        Upon their dark dazzle of needles,

Their mineral buckets and ore-boats
Like millwheels, pinnacling, restoring lightly
All over me from the green mines
And black-holes of the family plot.
                                    I am one of them
            For as long as we all shall die
And be counted.   I am the one this late morning
Pulled-through alive: the one frame-humming, conveying
                                        the tension,
            Black-browed from the black-holes
Of family peace.   My uncle's brows are still
As they were, growing out in mine,
                                    and I rest with good gut-
            feel in the hand-loomed bright-out,
In the dead's between-stitches breathing,
And am watchful as to what I do
With the swirl-cut of my straight look,
And of whom among the living it shall fix
With trembling, with unanswerable logic,
With green depth and short deadly grasses,

With my dead full-time and work-singing.

II

In Lace and Whalebone

            Bull-headed, big-busted,
Distrustful and mystical: my summoned kind of looks
            As I stand here going back
And back, from mother to mother: I am totally them in the
                                        eyebrows,
Breasts, breath and butt:
                  You, never-met Grandmother of the fields
            Of death, who laid this frail dress

Most freshly down, I stand now in your closed bones,
Sucked-in, in your magic tackle, taking whatever,

From the stark freedom under the land,
From under the sea, from the bones of the deepest beast,
Shaped now entirely by me, by whatever
Breath I draw.   I smell of clear

Hope-surfeited cedar: ghost-smell and forest-smell
Laid down in dim vital boughs
And risen in lace
and a feeling of nakedness is broadening
world-wide out
From me ring on ring—a refining of open-work skin—to go
With you, and I have added
Bad temper, high cheek-bones and exultation:
I fill out these ribs

For something ripped-up and boiled-down,
Plundered and rendered, come over me
From a blanched ruck of thorned, bungled blubber,
From rolling ovens raking-down their fires

For animal oil, to light room after room
In peculiar glister, from a slim sculpt of blown-hollow crystal:
Intent and soft-fingered
Precipitous light, each touch to the wick like drawing
First blood in a great hounded ring
the hand blunted and gone
Fathomless, in rose and ash, and cannot throw
The huddled burn out of its palm:

It is all in the one breath, as in the hush
Of the hand: the gull stripped downwind, sheering off
To come back slow,
the squandered fat-trash boiling in the wake,
The weird mammalian bleating of bled creatures,

A thrall of ships:
            lyric hanging of rope
(The snarled and sure entanglement of space),
Jarred, hissing squalls, tumultuous yaw-cries
Of butchery, stressed waves that part, close, re-open
Then seethe and graze: I hold-in my lungs
And hand, and try-out the blood-bones of my mothers,
And I tell you they are volcanic, full of exhorted hoverings:
                                    This animal:
        This animal: I stand and think

Its feed   its feel   its whole lifetime on one air:
        In lightning-strikes I watch it leap
And welter   blue wide-eyes   lung-blood up-misting under
    Stamped splits of astounding concentration,
    But soundless,
                    the crammed wake blazing with fat
    And phosphor,
                    the moon stoning down, Venus rising,

        And we can hold, woman on woman,
    This dusk if no other
                    and we will now, all of us combining,
            Open one hand.
                            Blood into light

Is possible: lamp, lace and tackle   paired bones of the deep
    Rapture
                surviving   reviving, and wearing well
            For this sundown, and not any other,
            In the one depth

        Without levels, deepening for us.

Concerning the Book *Puella* and Two of Its Poems

Puella consists of nineteen poems which attempt to "male-imagine" some of the changes, reactions, rituals, fantasies, wish fulfillments, aggrandizements, disappointments, guilt feelings and hidden exultations of a young girl moving from late childhood through puberty. The inner life of such a girl, strangely hers, entirely hers, too dreamlike and too real at the same time, was the life of any young girl I could imagine, and since when I began I had recently married a woman less than half my age, there could be no way in which my thinking of her, around her, through her, and by means of her could not be part of what I was doing. There was also what I conceived to be a new method, a new approach involved. I had for some time wanted to get away from the situation-poem, the poem whose principle element is narrative, the Aristotelian beginning-middle-and-end poem, the metered anecdote. I felt that language was capable of doing, perhaps even in my hands, a good deal more than I had been asking of it, and I wanted to try for an atmosphere of connotative release, and to place an aura of implication around the words that would show the entities depicted by the poem as in a clear deep liquid or mist, if possible glowing, seen in a kind of intimate distance that would at the same time have the density of interior life. Here, there are circumstances which one might construe as dramatic, or at least as so intended, but I did not wish the reader to feel that actions and events are asserted as the main things, nor did I wish reality to be felt as the obvious visible one. Over all these poems lay a willingness—a *will*—to follow Mallarmé's injunction to "give the initiative to *words*." Consequently the poems are more subjective than any others I have written, and perhaps for some readers more obscure, count-

ing as they do on suggestion rather than statement, or on inci-
dents and occasions declared. Literarily, as nearly as I can tell,
the closest ancestors of *Puella* are Rilke's Orpheus sonnets,
Mallarmé's *Hérodiade*, and Valéry's *Jeune Parque*, particularly
the last. These poems and poets are strictly ideals; *Puella* has
no formal kinship to any of them, hoping only for the other
affinity; spiritual, maybe.

In the two poems called "Deborah as Scion" the protago-
nist tries to assess the new mystery of her appearance; that is,
as we say in a different but quite the same connection, her
looks. At first dimly and then sharply, seizingly and associa-
tionally she realizes that her appearance has something—
everything—to do with the people in her family before her,
especially the women, all the way back. Simultaneously, as
she concentrates on what—and who—lives in her features and
her body, she becomes aware of the dead in a new way. In the
first poem she finds herself looking down on them in the fam-
ily plot of a cemetery, where they lie in their "oblong, thrilling
frame-tension / Filled here with sunlight." Lying thus, the
graves are now also felt as giving off another kind of light,
person-filled, family-owned, which rises to her and be-
queaths her features, bold, thick-eyebrowed and straight-at-
you. Some of her better characteristics, such as her solidity
and physical strength, come from the working-class back-
ground of her people, or certain of them, and at the end of the
first section she senses her forebears both working and sing-
ing in her as she stands above them and the "short deadly
grasses" where they labor like harvesters or miners or mill
hands to cause her to live, to stand above them in that shape
and those features.

The second part, "In Lace and Whalebone," is concerned
initially also with appearance, this time with dress, as the girl
wonders how real ancestral clothing—a grandmother's wed-
ding dress—would look on her; or, perhaps more important,
how she would look in it. I tried to deal with the universal fe-
male propensity to try on clothes; the girl wants not only to
wear the grandmother's garments from the skin out, to see
what whalebone stays would look and feel like, but to get
some notion of what they would, maybe, "do for her." When

she stands before the mirror, encased in whalebone, in the fir-scented and old-fashioned but perhaps not unbecoming lace, she enters fully into a fantasy about the means by which the stays were obtained, the bones of "the deepest beast" in which she now stands, breathless from the pressure, self-admiring, and is carried beyond her likeness into the imagined violence, under an overclouded, lightning-riddled sky, of the death of the whale whose bones are holding her, and "witnesses" the harpooning of the animal "in a great hounded ring," the arena-ed huge floundering blood of the blue-eyed creature, becoming cognizant now of the whole whaling operation, the bloody work-process, as she fills out the ribs

> For something ripped-up and boiled-down,
> Plundered and rendered, come over me
> From a blanched ruck of thorned, bungled blubber,
> From rolling ovens raking-down their fires

> For animal oil, to light room after room
> In peculiar glister. . . .

With the reference to lamps she moves into quietness and an awareness of the domestic past: a setting lit by whale oil and inhabited by her mothers, backward and backward: all her female kin in their bride-beds and birth-beds and death-beds in the dim light given off by an animal, and she understands now that indeed there has been, there can be, "blood into light." As she holds her breath as though under water, in the "paired bones of the deep / Rapture" she is holding also the breath of her mothers and that of all the family dead, with "the moon stoning down, Venus rising," and understands that she too is one in the life cycle with the others, that every sundown is every death, that, as Melville says, "life still dies sunward, full of faith," and, with her other women, with her family, she is "in the one depth / Without levels, deepening for us," and glad to be there.

STEPHEN DOBYNS

Cemetery Nights

Sweet dreams, sweet memories, sweet taste of earth:
here's how the dead pretend they're still alive—
one drags up a chair, a lamp, unwraps
the newspaper from somebody's garbage,
then sits holding the paper up to his face.
No matter if the lamp is busted and his eyes
have fallen out. Or some of the others
group together in front of the TV, chuckling
and slapping what's left of their knees.
No matter if the screen is dark. Four more
sit at a table with glasses and plates,
lift forks to their mouths and chew. No matter
if their plates are empty and they chew only air.
Two of the dead roll on the ground,
banging and rubbing their bodies together
as if in love or frenzy. No matter if their skin
breaks off, that their genitals are just a memory.

The head cemetery rat calls in all the city rats
who pay him what rats find valuable—
the wing of a pigeon or ear of a dog.
The rats perch on tombstones and the cheap
statues of angels and, oh, they hold their bellies
and laugh, laugh until their guts half break;
while the stars give off the same cold light
that all these dead once planned their lives by,
and in someone's yard a dog barks and barks
just to see if some animal as dumb as he is
will wake from sleep and perhaps bark back.

Communication

Sometimes I think communication is all we have—a voice like a silver wire extending through the dark or one chunk of flesh pressing against another chunk of flesh. Sometimes I don't even think that.

But when I believe in communication, I think this is the best way out of our self-absorption and isolation. By communication I mean not only a consciously intended verbal exchange of ideas and/or feelings but also an openness to the possibility of that exchange. Certainly there is a lot of nonintentional or unconscious communication, but that is not so much an exchange as a form of barking. The air is always full of barking; that's part of the trouble.

It seems to me that a work of art has the potential for being the highest form of communication. It can remove us from our essential isolation and join us in a community of shared human experience. It can show us that our most private feelings are in fact common feelings. Art is an antidote to madness. It allows us to define ourselves with greater or lesser accuracy in relation to our fellow human beings. Furthermore, great art, by showing us our common feeling, shows us our common responsibility. It shows us how to live.

It is thinking that art has the potential for being the highest form of communication that enables me to write poems. It forms an ideal that I strive for. When I stop believing in the possibility of that communication, then I don't write. Why bother? The construction of the poem purely for the sake of the poem gives me no pleasure. It turns the poem into a kind of decoration, something akin to wallpaper.

Mostly I think there is no communication. When I talk to someone, what I often seem to hear is "I want, I want more, I am lonely, I hurt, I am unhappy." Besides that, there may also be the need to compete, to dominate, or to diminish. And me too, I think, I must be doing the same thing. Here I am under the impression that I'm talking about Art, Truth, or Beauty, and instead I am jockeying for position while making little barks of need.

These are the active interferences with communication. There may also be passive interferences: indifference or the inability to listen. There is that moment in Chekhov's "The Lady with The Dog" when Dimitry wants to tell someone about this woman whom he doesn't even yet know that he loves. So he says to a card-playing friend as they leave their club, "If you only knew what a charming woman I met in Yalta." And his friend, after getting into his sleigh, responds, "You were quite right, Dimitry—the sturgeon was just a little bit off."

So I have two opposing beliefs that exist side by side—one, that communication is possible; two, that it is impossible— and I swing back and forth, writing or not writing. But even while communication is difficult, art is a way of making it palatable. Instead of saying, "If you only knew what a charming woman I met at Yalta," you work it into a short story or poem or sonata. And what I find is that while the poem may begin with my little concerns, it finally, if it is successful, transcends my concerns. This is very liberating. Even if not communicated, the concerns have been shed. And so this becomes one of the many reasons why I write.

This brings us to "Cemetery Nights," which I began in November 1982. It was the first new poem I had written in about ten months. Instead of writing new poems, I had been finishing my fourth book of poems, Black Dog, Red Dog, which meant doing a lot of rewriting. I was also working on several novels.

But I also felt somewhat disillusioned with poetry, my own and all the others'. In Black Dog, Red Dog, I had tried writing realistic narratives, mostly using a twelve- to fourteen-syllable line while manipulating the line breaks to maintain tension. But by early 1982, I had come to an end of it. Furthermore, I had spent six months in Santiago, Chile, and was beginning to believe that realism was an inadequate mode for dealing with the world's excesses; or rather, a realistic approach came across as fantastic—what people who know nothing about surrealism call surrealistic. I also felt (partly because of Chile) that I had to try harder to write poems that engaged with the world. It seems obvious that we are going to blow up the world, and I wanted whatever I wrote to be enmeshed with that sense of our future. Also, it embarrassed me that Europeans and Latin Americans had endless scorn for American poems—poetry where the writer does little more than say, I have a little pain.

What I wanted was to begin a new book of poems, and I wanted it to be as different from *Black Dog, Red Dog* as that book was from *The Balthus Poems.* The model I had in mind, although I didn't go back to look at his work, was the drawings and watercolors of George Grosz in his *Ecce Homo,* since in the American solipsism of the 1980s, I thought I saw resemblances with Berlin of the 1920s. Additionally, I liked the way he distorted the realistic into the fantastic, yet kept the impression of realism.

I had also been reading a lot of Baudelaire, his essays as well as his poems, and it seemed that one of the factors that allowed him to get away with the harshness of his subject matter was the extreme rigor of his form. I had experimented slightly with a tighter form in *Black Dog, Red Dog,* especially in the poem "Bleeder," which deals with the desire to make a hemopheliac bleed. There I had used a loose blank verse and had liked how the increased tension accentuated yet helped to control the emotion. Consequently, in moving toward a new book, I decided to use a vague *vers libéré** instead of purely free verse—to move back and forth between an iambic and free-verse ten-syllable line. Along with this, I wanted to use more traditionally formal devices but use them unpredict-

---

*French prosody distinguishes between *vers libre* and *vers libéré,* that is between verse that is completely free and verse that is partly free yet still contains an element of meter. It is what T.S. Eliot was advocating when he said that "the ghost of some simple metre should lurk behind the arras in even the 'freest' verse; to advance menacingly as we doze, and withdraw as we rouse. Or, freedom is only truly freedom when it appears against the background of artificial limitation."

ably so that the rhythmic and aural direction of the poem could not be correctly anticipated.

So these were some of my concerns. Yet I had no poem, had not written a new poem for ten months and was currently going through a period of thinking that communication was impossible. All I knew was what I wanted to do, while also wanting to shake the feeling of futility.

The poem came from deciding to make that idea—the belief in the futility of communication—into the subject of a poem: a neat paradox. The actual poem evolved from joining together three sets of images. The image of the dead in the first stanza derives from Stanley Spencer's Judgement Day paintings, where the dead are seen crawling out of their coffins in an English village. The image of the rats came in part from a metaphor found in W. S. Merwin's *Asian Figures:* "Talk about tomorrow and the rats will laugh." As for the dog, I think that image of the howling or barking dog has always been with me, and I use it again and again. Here it came to signify that sense of the futility of communication which was keeping me from writing. The barking dog in the third to last line is the poem itself. The poet, if he exists in the poem at all, is probably the "someone" who owns the yard. The dog doesn't want an answer. It wants acknowledgment of its existence. What's the point of saying, "Me, me, me," unless someone can hear you?

These three images had been circling with others in my head. Along with them was the idea that no matter how ugly life is, it is still sweet. Along with that was the desire to make a certain sound: to again and again begin a loose iambic rhythm, then break it. Simplistically, that is how I write a poem. I have a number of aural, emotional, and intellectual concerns floating along with a series of images like flies circling in the center of a room. I repeat the rhythms and sounds in my head, run through the images as if through a tray of slides, and lean against the concerns as one might lean against a closed door.

The poem comes when I am suddenly able to join these concerns together under the aegis of one idea or feeling. Here it was the futility of communication, and I suppose at its most basic level the poem is about my coping with writer's block. Once the elements are joined, the rough shape of the poem comes very quickly. Then I spend months straightening it out and trying to become entirely conscious of the meaning, while moving the poem away from my personal concerns (writer's block) to a more general concern (the need and desire for communication).

What is now the first line of the poem was actually the last to be written. The second line (originally the first) is an iambic pentameter line beginning with what is almost a spondee. The present third line is also iambic pentameter, although the first unstressed syllable has been dropped. Lines 4 and 5 move away from the iambic, while the ''no matter'' in line 6 entirely disrupts the iambic movement. This was to be the movement of the first stanza—a constant playing with iambic pentameter and breaking it four times with the repetition of ''no matter,'' which itself becomes a rhythmic device.

A main error in my early version was to assume that the reason for the dead's actions was clear—that by mimicking the daily actions of their lives they were attempting to recover a bit of the sweetness. Fortunately, I showed the poem to a friend who said, ''But why do the dead do that?'' So I added the first line, which also enabled me to increase the rhythmic tension by making the line iambic pentameter. Three of those iambs, however, are near spondees, and their placement gave me the chance to emphasize a pattern of spondees or near spondees in the first stanza—sixteen occur in those original sixteen lines. By building up a pattern of double stresses, I wanted to prepare for the series of triple stresses which closes the poem. There are also other patterns in the first stanza—a move between high-frequency vowels (*ee*) and low-frequency vowels (*ou*), a move between hard consonants (*b, d, g, p, t*) and soft consonants (*ch, f, th*).

The rats don't really realize what is going on. I suppose they represent me at my most cynical—believing that communication is impossible, that the whole mess is pointless. They don't understand that the dead are only trying to catch a taste of sweetness. It's the act itself which is important, not what comes of it. The rats, after all, are predators and scavengers—

they only think in terms of gain. They can't imagine staring at a blank TV screen just for the memory it elicits, of getting some sweetness from the illusion. As the poem says, it doesn't matter that the TV is dark.

The image of the stars in lines 6 and 7 was a fortuitous discovery, although stars are another image which I tend to overuse. In any case, I needed a bridge to get to the dog and I thought how the dead, when young, had planned their lives under the same starlight that now glimmers above their antics. But I saw that that doesn't matter, that what is important is to have a life even if it's a dumb one. What enables one to live is the most rudimentary form of hope. The barking dog, for all its foolishness, is a symbol of such hope.

Rhythmically, the second stanza resembles the first, but its pattern of ten spondees is further heightened by six triple stresses. The most obvious triple stresses are those ending lines 6, 7, and 11, while that last line is further intensified by a strong iambic beat. The line length in this stanza generally decreases to nine syllables, and there are a higher number of hard consonants. All this was intended to make the stanza more compact, move faster, and seem more desperate, while the repeat of the triple stress at the end was meant to give a conclusion similar to a piece of music.

As a change from earlier work, what I liked best about the poem was its tone—dealing with the fantastic in a matter-of-fact manner, using flat assertion and perfectly plain description. I was also attempting to use this tone in my fiction, and although I was drawn to it in Apollinaire, I thought I saw it best used in the fiction of Gabriel García Márquez. Yet he had partly learned it from Faulkner, and in thinking about that tone I went back to Faulkner to try to re-create the slow-paced, highly detailed, matter-of-fact relating of fantastic events—say, a horse galloping through a house.

It seems each successful poem must challenge and overcome the complacency of a reader. Before beginning this poem, I had a number of concerns which were further emphasized by my desire to change the direction of my work. I myself was becoming complacent with the methods and strategies I had used in *Black Dog, Red Dog* and felt it was time to stir up the pot. The desire to use a new tone, humor, elements of the fantastic, a tighter form, use less personal material, use direct speech, abrupt juxtapositions and surprise, to write a more aggressive poem—all these concerns I had defined to myself in a six-month period before writing the poem. Then all I could do was wait for that coming together of image, idea, emotion, and language. It also took that shift in attitude—the belief that communication is possible. Still, people can barely talk together. The fact that we are on the very brink of nuclear holocaust seems the clearest evidence of this. Personally, I think there is about one chance out of a hundred that we'll get through the century without doing ourselves in.

I think a poem has the ability to sensitize a person toward himself and the world around him. As Suzanne Langer says, a work of art is the objectification of subjective life. It gives form to inward experience and makes it conceivable. It helps a person to define himself in relation to the world and even predict the course of that world. For me, this makes each poem a political act and, even though I expect no results from these political acts, it keeps me writing. There is another Asian Figure which I often quote to myself: ''Sardine threatens, who knows it?'' But writing poems is what I do best and so I keep doing it. It is also what I like to do best. Clearly, my definitions as to the function of poetry are connected to the series of definitions that allow me to tolerate myself, let me get up each morning and not put a bullet in my head. That finally is why I keep coming back to thinking that communication might be possible. Not only does it allow me to write, it keeps me alive.

CAROLYN FORCHÉ

Endurance

In Belgrade, the windows of the tourist
hotel opened over seven storeys of lilacs,
rain clearing sidewalk tables of linens
and liquor, the silk flags of the non-
aligned nations like colorful underthings
pinned to the wind. Tito was living.
I bought English, was mistaken for Czech,
walked to the fountains, the market
of garlic and tents, where I saw
my dead Anna again and again,
hard yellow beans in her lap,
her babushka of white summer cotton,
her eyes the hard pits of her past.
She was gossiping among her friends,
saying the rosary or trying to sell me
something. Anna. Peeling her hands
with a paring knife, saying *in your country
you having nothing.* Each word was the husk
of a vegetable tossed to the street
or a mountain rounded by trains
with cargoes of sheep-dung and grief.
I searched in Belgrade for some holy
face painted *without hands* as when
an ikon painter goes to sleep and awakens
with an image come from the dead.
On each corner Anna dropped
her work in her lap and looked up.
I am a childless poet, I said.
I have not painted an egg, made prayers
or finished my Easter duty in years.
I left Belgrade for Frankfurt last
summer, Frankfurt for New York,

New York for the Roanoke valley
where mountains hold the breath
of the dead between them and lift
from each morning a fresh bandage of mist.
New York, Roanoke, the valley—
to this Cape where in the dunes
the wind takes a body of its own
and a fir tree comes to the window
at night, tapping on the glass like
a woman who has lived too much.
Piskata, hold your tongue, she says.
I am trying to tell you something.

A Fantasy of Birches

Each night Anna trudged from the house to the field's edge with her sack of garbage. Dead weeds rattled over the blue snow as she made her fire in the iron can, lighting it with a swipe of a kitchen match. Here she prayed in Slovak, supposedly burning the trash while she watched her fire, jabbing a spray of red stars from the bin with her stick. Sometimes I went with her. At these times she talked on a variety of subjects, such as life in the old country and the facts of sex. *Piskata*, she would say, *it looks like a sausage.*

One night in summer she carried my dolls back there, explaining that childhood was an American invention and I was too old to play with monkeys. I pulled them out of the fire before their dresses had caught. Another time she tried to teach me how to have crows land on my head as they did on hers while she fed them rye scraps. Such were the origins of my ambivalence toward her.

She was born Anna Bassar on May 14, 1883, in a village called Tarnov twenty miles from Bratislava. It is said that she stowed away on a ship when she was nine and didn't return to her family for two years, insisting that she'd seen the world. In 1899 she came to America with her parents; they worked in the cotton mills of New Hartford, Connecticut—she in the shining room, her father in the card mill. Four years later she married Michael Joseph Sidlosky, a Slovak from Forbas, Hungary, who thinking mill work was for weak men, left with his wife for the coke ovens of Ohio. There he did the work later assigned to two, smoothing the hot coke with a rake. The coke plant gave them a boardinghouse to manage, called the "hobnail house" because of the clatter of nails pounded into the soles to preserve their shoes. Anna made the boarders take turns sleeping on and under the beds—she spoke Slovak and Romanian to them, and cooked Slavic and

Mennonite foods. Her language was a cassoulet of Polish slang and Slovak, Yiddish, Hungarian and Czech. The foods I grew up to believe were eastern European were actually Mennonite. Fed up one day she announced to Michael Joseph that she was going back to the Connecticut mills until he found her a house of their own. Her parents had wearied and returned to Slovakia for the rest of their offspring. When they came back they were turned away from Ellis Island because of an open sore on her father's leg.

Anna spoke peasant Slovak well and English poorly. When she wanted a colander, for example, she said, "*Piskata,* go get me the macaroni-stop-water-go-head." So I was able to learn the personal invention of language. For this gift, Anna has in the years since her death determined to be included in any book of poems I might complete. *I want to be in the book,* she says, standing behind me in a room late at night, leaning on her old potato shovel. Many Sunday afternoons of my childhood were command assemblies of her many descendants for pinochle and food in the yard behind the house in Detroit. One does not refuse the matriarch.

"*Piskata,* in the old country there are no weeds in the woods. Not like you have here, all this junk between the trees! Just a nice carpet of grass." This while she swept the sawdust from the garage. My father had been building a dollhouse for my monkeys after work. "This country is a piece of shit," she added. I asked my father about this political observation while he was trying to cut a perfect mansard doll roof on the circular saw. "Shut up," he explained. The idea of the woods remained with me.

During the Cuban missile crisis, Anna received an urgent letter from her sister in Slovakia, announcing that her sons, who were in the Czech army, had been shipped to Cuba by the Soviets. "It is only a few miles away from America," my great-aunt wrote, "and so I want you to go there and pick them up. They are your nephews! At least you should meet them."

"You can't go to Cuba," my mother explained, in the tone she reserved for Anna.

"Why is everyone so upset around here?" my siblings

asked. As the oldest, I urged them in a bossy whisper to go hide under their beds. Anna was prevented.

She sewed polka dresses for us trimmed with rickrack that made us look, my mother thought, like we just got off the boat. ''You are *Americans*,'' she told us over and over.

Anna roamed. When she wasn't punching bread dough, thumbing her prayer book, weeping over her losses, or gathering the polka dress scraps into quilts, she climbed in her old white Mercury and disappeared for weeks, going back to the coke oven and cotton mill towns, staying on the road with strangers who even now show up at her children's houses in Detroit, saying they are Anna's friends. At seventy-eight she vanished for seven weeks, returning to announce she'd found herself a second husband.

It was a stormy marriage. John Holda repaired clocks, and so the walls were filled with cuckoos and chimes, tiny men who pounded each other hourly over the head with mallets. Every quarter hour the house chirped, half-hourly the bells sounded, moment to moment the pendulums clicked in their glass cabinets. We searched the glittering clockworks on his lamplit table, looking for the tiny jewels he said were always included. It is said that Anna soon reached the limit of her small patience, dropping several clocks from a second-storey window and issuing the others to friends. For the rest of his days, John Holda took the same few clocks apart over and over.

I remember the steel light, the phone wire of perched birds, the quiet drive with my father to Anna's deathbed through fields coated with rime ice. We each approached her and spoke our names. She passed from the slow dictation of details for her funeral into the whispered language of her childhood and a fruit-breathed silence. She had even decided which of the women would bring what dish for the party— this one a good pirohy, that one the pastry we called angel wings. She had named her pallbearers, chosen the music and priest; she would return in death to the side of her first husband, on the hill overlooking their Leetonia farmhouse.

She went into the ground in her Sunday clothes without a babushka, holding her rosary beads, the coffin covered with chrysanthemums. The Slovak spoken in our home was lowered into the ground with her. I wasn't old enough to have asked her the most important questions, although I imagine she would have answered these with a request to melt some lard, wash the draining boards, or get out of the way. Four years later, in a poem by Derek Walcott, I discovered another Anna.

your back, bent at its tasks, in the blue kitchen,
or hanging flags of laundry, feeding the farm's chickens,
against a fantasy of birches . . .

foreign as snow,
far away as first love,
my Akhmatova!

Twenty years later, in the odour of burnt shells,
you can remind me of "A Visit to the Pasternaks,"
so that you are suddenly the word "wheat,"

falling on the ear, against the frozen silence of a weir,
again you are bending
over a cabbage garden, tending
a snowdrift of rabbits,
or pulling down the clouds from the thrumming
   clotheslines

If dreams are signs,
then something died this minute,
its breath blown from a different life . . .

You are suddenly old, white-haired,
like the herons, the turned page. Anna, I wake
to the knowledge that things sunder
from themselves, like peeling bark. *

*Another Life (New York: Farrar, Straus & Giroux, 1973), pp. 97–98.

Years later, when I entered what I believed my adulthood as a poet, I wrote "Burning the Tomato Worms" for her. The title arose from the method she used to eliminate the green worms that chew tomato leaves and vines. Most would use a pesticide, or pull the worms away with a stick. Anna lit a match under each one she found, holding it far enough away that the worm slowly warmed and rose on its hind legs to wave in the air before bursting, to her delighted clapping of hands. She passed the box to me to assume this task behind her, usually in the early morning when the sky was still pink over Detroit. In those bird-filled hours I learned the loathing of worms and the silence of work. She was followed down the rows of tomatoes by crows she cursed in Slovak.

"Write what you feel compelled to write," someone later told me. The advice rescued my poems and pleased Anna.

A decade intervened between her death and my departure to work in El Salvador in 1978. The poems which insisted upon themselves were of that country: the earliest a letter to the Salvadoran exiled poet Claribel Alegria, another to a prisoner who guided me through thirty minutes in a prison in Ahuachapan. The others were poems of dislocation, a mirror of Anna's mysterious childhood quest to know the world, which in 1978 took me to Yugoslavia during a conference of the Non-Aligned Nations in Belgrade. My room was on the seventh floor of the Hotel Tourist, the windows opening to a grey slab of terrace edged with flowering lilacs like those Anna tended, chopping bouquets with her meat knife to scent the house. After Salvador, I was unnerved by the single door to my room and kept it chain-locked, and by the open window through which, in a more dangerous country, one might be thrown. In my insomnia I escaped into what few English books I could find, and during the hot hours walked the mirage of a shimmering grey city, taking notes at outdoor cafe tables and noticing in the face of each old woman in the market the face of Anna Sidlosky Holda. A few seemed to recognize me as well, or such was my imagination. In their Serbian I heard fragments of her Slovak. On one vertiginous walk through the streets, a worker-housing complex seemed to move slightly to the left and back in a faint wind. I wanted to leave Belgrade, and a friend offered a trip to Zlatibor, a village in the Serbian mountains some hours by train, where the partisan poet Vasko Vukasavlovic lived with his wife, Stolyanka.

We packed bread, fruit, and a goatskin of wine, and the train pulled through Valjevo into the Serbian countryside: a man pitching straw, a woman going to her gate with a basket of eggs. "A million and a half Yugoslavs died," my companion said, "in the camps. This country's losses were imponderable."

The compartment was close, the air ribboned with tobacco smoke; on and off I slept until we entered the mountains. Through the window, tinted amber with nicotine, I saw that there were no weeds in the Serbian woods but a nice carpet of grass between the trees. When this registered, I stood in the aisle, pounded on the shoulder of my friend, and cried, "There are no weeds in the woods!" The woman beside us shook her head sadly, suggesting that the Amerikanska was too hot and should get air at the next stop. The sheep grazed between the trees, biting the growth to the quick. Anna had told the truth. "I'm in one of the old countries," I wrote in a notebook letter I would never be able to send, "and your memory of it is true." I wondered then what else. What more could I retrieve of what she had said about the world?

Her demand to be in the second book became the poem "Endurance." If I could speak with her again, it is what I would tell her. In every generation of Slovak women there had been one who wanders, restless-hearted, by ship or in an old car, and that measure of strange blood was passed this time to me. The poem is to tell her that I recognize her when she comes behind me as I write, talking about how much work there is to do, or, as she entered a wintering tree in Provincetown, seeming closer to the window each night until the icy branches tapped on the glass "like a woman who has lived too much." Her chidings in terms of the work to be done still reach me.

TESS GALLAGHER

Each Bird Walking

Not while, but long after he had told me,
I thought of him, washing his mother, his
bending over the bed and taking back
the covers. There was a basin of water
and he dipped a washrag in and
out of the basin, the rag
dripping a little onto the sheet as he
turned from the bedside to the nightstand
and back, there being no place

on her body he shouldn't touch because
he had to and she helped him, moving
the little she could, lifting so he could
wipe under her arms, a dipping motion
in the hollow. Then working up from
the feet, around the ankles, over the
knees. And this last, opening
her thighs and running the rag firmly
and with the cleaning thought
up through her crotch, between the lips,
over the V of thin hairs—

as though he were a mother
who had the excuse of cleaning to touch
with love and indifference,
the secret parts of her child, to graze
the sleepy sexlessness in its waiting
to find out what to do for the sake
of the body, for the sake of what only
the body can do for itself.

So his hand, softly at the place

of his birth-light. And she, eyes deepened
and closed in the dim room.
And because he told me her death as
important to his being with her,
I could love him another way. Not
of the body alone, or of its making,
but carried in the white spires of trembling
until what spirit, what breath we were
was shaken from us. Small then,
the word *holy*.

He turned her on her stomach
and washed the blades of her shoulders, the
small of the back. "That's good," she said,
"that's enough."
On our lips that morning, the tart juice
of the mothers, so strong in remembrance, no
asking, no giving, and what you said, this
being the end of our loving, so as not to hurt
the closer one to you, made me look
to see what was left of us
with our sex taken away. "Tell me," I said,
"something I can't forget." Then the story of
your mother, and when you finished
I said, "That's good, that's enough."

Sing It Rough

There are aspects of the writer-reader relationship which sometimes drive a poet into apology and denial. Readers, of course, are more likely to put their faith in a piece of writing when they can feel there's a reasonable explanation for the choices the writer is making. They want order and magic at once. But the magic of poetry so often works against the taxidermy of logic and the reasoned apprehension of experience, that the poet turns outlaw when the reader wants to bulldog a poem into one-two-three-four meaning.

One of the stories I've found myself telling to explain the mystery out of the title, ''Each Bird Walking,'' does, I think, have a good deal to do with the interiors of the poem. When I was a child I used to chase pigeons while my mother paused to chat with friends she encountered on our shopping trips into town. I wanted desperately to catch a pigeon, just one, to see what a pigeon felt like to hold. My mother would buy some fresh popcorn from the dime store and I would tempt the pigeons round and round the parking meters until clouds of birds had carried off the last puff and kernel I had to offer. Although I was never once successful, I kept thinking that, finally, with the right agility and stealth, I would eventually lay hands on a pigeon. I assumed from the start that birds must be of a higher order than people. Birds could fly over entire towns and forests. The gulls of this seaport could not only fly, but could alight on water or fly up into the hemlocks. Why shouldn't I think birds were miracles? But there was also this curious two-footed walking around they did. As I flung out my popcorn week after week, I puzzled on this: why, if they could fly, did birds bother to come down at all and walk around the ankles of shopkeepers and children?

Then, in my perverse way, I began to think it wasn't so much the birds' flying that was exceptional, but this arduous walking, this dodging and skittering, this strutting and hop-flying, peck-walking they did among humans. Why humble themselves so if they could soar like angels?

In telling this story I manage to reawaken a sense of humor and an awareness of the miraculous in the readers who need reasons. They seem to remember what it is to have been a child and to have wanted to catch birds. Then I speak about the way in which birds have been identified as emblematic of the spirit in scriptural texts. Birds, according to Jungian chartings of the archetypal unconscious, have represented the spirit in countless ancient and not-so-ancient cultures. I remind my listeners, many of whom have not the slightest interest in either birds or the archetypal unconscious, that birds have often been represented as the message bearers of gods. When a spirit leaves a body, I add, it was sometimes seen to do so in the shape of a bird, often a dove. I feel myself getting perilously close to "the point." And, of course, the closer I get to making it—the point—the more I want to tell yet another story about birds and childhood. Then, before I can stop myself, I have said: "Sometimes the spirit, like a bird, has to walk, has to humble itself and do the unassuming, ordinary, necessary, the daily thing in order to attend most to its life and the lives of others." "Each Bird Walking" is a title that doesn't explain, but illuminates the poem in the way a kite tells us the currents of wind by its swoops and feints toward earth.

"But there are no birds in your poem."

I have to hear this remark because the speaker has cupped her hands into a megaphone and is standing like a karate expert, feet wide apart in the aisle. No, there are no birds in my poem. There is a son, a mother, and a speaker. They are each doing the painful but matter-of-fact caretaking that must be done, and this doesn't look miraculous, though it is. The son is walking, is calmly going about the step-by-step motions of attending a life on its way to death. The speaker walks in the sense of knowing that this love must end, yet must be carried into memory with dignity and meaning. In the title, the mention of birds walking reads like the attraction of place-names called out on a train in a foreign country, countries that will remain foreign. You can't get off the train to investigate, but an aura of excitement surrounds each of the names. You know they are the right and only names to designate exactly those places. You don't know why, but you know.

One of the things this poem generates, besides questions for which there are no satisfactory answers, is a need for storytelling. I have been amazed at how many men from audiences have come up to me after hearing the poem and have told how they've nursed their fathers, wives, or brothers through final days and nights. There is something composed and humble about these men who feel invited by the poem to share with me. Their tenderness shines forth. The world is richer.

When a taboo is broken there is often the feeling of freshness, a freeing of breath as it rushes in. Because I tell this story of a son and his mother, I break the ancient taboo against touching between mother and son. Throughout the course of civilization women have been the caretakers of the body during birth, illness, and death. The poem, by showing a man in this role, enlarges the share men may have in this experience.

There is nothing technically exceptional about the poem. Its poetry, in a very specific sense, resides partly in its challenge of the convention that sons may not intimately approach the bodies of their mothers after puberty. In a more general sense, it is the conception and presentation of a new arena of feeling and being which makes for poetry, a poetry concerned with forms of value in our lives. The gift of this poem, then, is the communal lifting of barriers to love—even if only for this deathbed ritual where it can hardly be refused. Also, by showing this son ministering to the mother, the poem returns positive energy to the mother-son relationship, which has most often been represented as claustrophobic and deserving of much agility on the part of sons in order to remain dutiful but distant, affectionate but rarely loving and certainly never devoted.

The speaker, the "I" of the poem, stays purposefully in the background. I say purposefully because the speaker is most valuable as witness here. Perhaps this humility of approach carries the reserve of emotion we know the speaker obeys in

the last words of the poem: "That's good, that's enough."
The ending places value in the idea of knowing when the
good has come to its fruition, of accepting its end as fulfill-
ment and not as deprivation or injury. This withholding of the
"I" allows the reader a larger participation in the acts of the
poem. The description of the washing is done in such a way
that the goodness and beauty of the act happen as if to the
reader as well as to the mother. The reader imaginatively as-
sociates with the body of the mother and is cleansed by the
words of the poem. The reader also becomes the speaker of
the poem, who must give over the intimacy of touch for the
intimacy of telling. Perhaps there is illumination, too, in the
reversal of roles: the son as mother, returning the care he's re-
ceived as an infant; the mother completing her life in the
needfulness she began with, the needfulness with which each
of us begins.

Although the poem is scrupulously nonsexual in its lan-
guage and intent, it is, for me in the telling, an extremely sen-
sual poem, a poem which caresses and honors the body. The
senses are at once stimulated by the recognition of the taboo
at the unconscious level, yet normalized by the explicit, sacra-
mental detailing and pacing of the poem. At the close of the
poem, we are carried beyond the physical as the story opens
into the ongoing memory of the speaker and consequently en-
ters the memory of the reader.

Because I have disappeared into "story" in the writing of
the poem, the language also disappears, does not call atten-
tion to itself. Its exactness comes from the authenticity of its
tone, its empathy with its characters and their acts, and the
urgency of felt knowledge working at an intuitive level to
make this occasion unforgettable. As Wendell Berry has
said, "Things that mattered to me once / won't matter any
more, / for I have left the safe shore where magnificence of
art / could suffice my heart." For me, this does not mean
that one does not choose the right words or forgets that a
poem is also music. It means there are always things at
stake in the poem that make demands which artifice alone
cannot deliver. As a singer and musician friend of mine,
Cahíl McConnel, says:

You can sing sweet
and get the song sung
but to get to the third
dimension you have to sing it
rough, hurt the tune a little. Put
enough strength to it
that the notes slip. Then
something else happens. The song
gets large.

This hurting of the tune is crucial for my growth as a writer now, for I've known all along how to "sing sweet." Certainly there are legions who're singing sweet, hitting all the expected notes at the right intervals. But how to hit the wrong notes because that's where the feeling takes you and because you have to go there or lose your life—the meaningfulness and intensity of this kind of struggle in the writing can't be carried by artifice. Call it heart. Call it gift and passion and courage of the sort that causes the poet's voice to inspire the reader with belief in the real and marvelous at once. Like that point which long-distance runners describe where the legs disappear, where the consciousness of legs dissolves, the spirit infuses language to the degree that it does not exist as separate from the activity—the telling, the singing, the giving over of the "I" to an energy *of* the self, yet beyond it.

The movement of the poem "Each Bird Walking" is toward a conjunction of partings: mother from son, son from mother, and lover from lover. The human miracle of the poem is that, unlike so many partings, this one did not end in damage and forgetting. Life attitude is as much and likely more a part of what makes for largesse in poetry than diction, voice, tone, or strategy. If I can't respect the motives and meanings *of* a poem—the values at work there—it matters little what pyrotechnics, what calisthenics of metaphor, of imagery or rhythm the writer displays.

"There's a live one," the poet Guillevic said to his interpreter as he shook the hand of someone he was meeting at a book signing in Killarney. He knew the current was on. The hand belonged to the living. It squeezed into his in such a way that the meeting took place. "Don't ghost it. Sing it rough," I tell myself heading into a poem. I want the meetings to take place, even after the book is closed and the poem is a thing remembered.

LOUISE GLÜCK

Night Song

Look up into the light of the lantern.
Don't you see? The calm of darkness
is the horror of heaven.

We've been apart too long, too painfully separated.
How can you bear to dream,
to give up watching? I think you must be dreaming,
your face is full of mild expectancy.

I need to wake you, to remind you that there isn't a future.
That's why we're free. And now some weakness in me
has been cured forever, so I'm not compelled
to close my eyes, to go back, to rectify—

The beach is still; the sea, cleansed of its superfluous life,
opaque, rocklike. In mounds, in vegetal clusters,
seabirds sleep on the jetty. Terns, assassins—

You're tired; I can see that.
We're both tired, we have acted a great drama.
Even our hands are cold, that were like kindling.
Our clothes are scattered on the sand; strangely enough,
they never turned to ashes.

I have to tell you what I've learned, that I know now
what happens to the dreamers.
They don't feel it when they change. One day
they wake, they dress, they are old.

Tonight I'm not afraid
to feel the revolutions. How can you want sleep
when passion gives you that peace?
You're like me tonight, one of the lucky ones.
You'll get what you want. You'll get your oblivion.

The Dreamer and The Watcher

I have to say at once that I am uneasy with this process. My insights on what I perceive to be the themes of this poem are already expressed: the poem embodies them. What I'm questioning is the value of the author's commentary. I can't add anything; what I can do is make the implicit explicit, which exactly reverses the poet's ambition. Perhaps the best alternative is to begin in circumstance.

In April of 1980, my house was destroyed by fire. A burned house: a reprimand to the collector. Gradually, certain benefits became apparent. I felt grateful; the vivid sense of escape conferred on daily life an aura of blessedness. I felt lucky to wake up, lucky to make the beds, lucky to grind the coffee. There was also, after a period of devastating grief, a strange exhilaration. Having nothing, I was no longer hostage to possessions. For six weeks, my husband and son and I lived with friends; in May, we moved into Plainfield village, which seemed, after the isolation of the country road, miraculously varied, alive.

At that time, I hadn't written anything for about six months. The natural silence after a book. Then the natural silence imposed by crisis. I was oddly at peace with it. What word did I use? Necessary, appropriate—whatever I said, the fact is that for once I relinquished the anxiety which, in my mind, ensured the return of vision. That first summer after the fire was a period of rare happiness. I mean, by that word, not ecstasy but another state, one more balanced, serene, attentive.

Toward the end of June, I began writing again, working on a poem called "Mock Orange." Then that poem was finished; in rapid succession, over a period of about two weeks, I wrote twelve more. Such experiences are, in many lives, a commonplace. But for me this was unprecedented and unexpectedly frightening. I kept feeling the poems weren't mine but collages of remembered lines. When I thought otherwise, I thought such fluency meant I was going to die, not sometime, but very soon. At such moments, for the first time in my life, I wished not to write; for the first time, I wanted survival above all else. That wish had no influence on behavior. Other factors—twenty years of discipline and obsession—were more powerful. When, of itself, the seizure ended, I was left with a sense of direction, a sense of how I wanted to sound. I wanted to locate poems in a *now* that would never recur, in a present that seemed to me utterly different from my previous uses of that tense. I had tried, always, to get at the unchanging. But, beginning at this time, my definitions of *essential* were themselves altering. I wanted, as well, poems not so much developed as undulant, more fire than marble. The work I'd just done suggested these possibilities. Meaning, it suggested a method, a tone. The chief attribute of that tone, as I heard it, was urgency, even recklessness. . . .

In practical terms, in the period before the fire I had set myself certain assignments. In the gloomy, unproductive winter of 1980, I was sorting, analyzing, trying to identify in my poems those habitual gestures—signature rhythms, tricks of syntax, and so on—that had to be discarded, trying, at the same time, to see what constructions I had tended to avoid. I had made a style of avoiding contractions and questions; it seemed to me I should learn to use them. Both forms felt completely alien, which was encouraging. That is, I allowed myself to believe something profound had been addressed. My work has always been strongly marked by a disregard for the circumstantial, except insofar as it could be transformed into paradigm. The poems in *Descending Figure* aim at a kind of terminal authority: they will not be distracted by the transitory, the partial; they reserve their love for what doesn't exist. I expect that, to some degree, this disposition not to acquiesce will always inform my work: an aspect of character. An aspect, also, of the passion for form. But if writing is to be a discovery, it must explore the unknown, and the unknown, to me, was informality—contractions and questions specify the human, not the oracular, voice.

"Night Song" was written in the early part of 1981, about six months after the period I've described. It's not clear to me to what extent the poem reflects either these concerns or these events. I find traces of both in the lines. And yet, the poem could not have been predicted. All this is something like looking at an old photograph of a friend: you can see readily how that child came to be this adult. But it doesn't work the other way; you can't find in the blurred, soft face of an infant the inevitable adult structure.

The process of writing doesn't, in my experience, vary much. What varies is the time required. For me, all poems begin in some fragment of motivating language—the task of writing a poem is the search for context. Other imaginations begin, I believe, in the actual, in the world, in some concrete thing which examination endows with significance. That process is generative: its proliferating associations produce a broad, lush, inclusive and, at times, playful poetry; its failures seem simply diffuse, without focus. My own work begins at the opposite end, at the end, literally, at illumination, which has then to be traced back to some source in the world. This method, when it succeeds, makes a thing that seems irrefutable. Its failure is felt as portentousness.

"Night Song" began with its first stanza, heard whole. And a working title: "Siren Song." A seduction. Are all seductions riddled with the imperative? As I remember, I had been thinking, on and off, of Psyche and Eros, thinking specifically of the illustration which had introduced these figures to me in childhood: the mortal woman bending over the ravishing god. This image remained with me, an independent fact, so divested of narrative that for years I didn't remember that Psyche had to be pressured into this betrayal. In my mind, Psyche leaning over Eros stood for the human compulsion to see, to know, for the rejection of whatever comfort results from deception. The figures suggested, as well, the dilemma of sexuality: the single body split apart again, an old subject; the exhausting obligation to recognize the other as other, as not part of the self.

For some months, I had no idea what to do with this beginning. The lines did seem a beginning: they were a summons, after all. In some sense, the "you" at this point was myself. "The calm of darkness is the horror of heaven"—the lesson was the lesson I keep trying to learn. But the poem had, I thought, to be dramatic.

When work resumed (how, why, I don't know), it went quickly. The dramatic situation remains sketchy—perhaps there is not enough background, in both senses of the word. But the truth is I didn't myself care about how these people got to this beach, or where the beach was. I could imagine no answers to such questions that were not conventional. What compelled me were the figures juxtaposed by this reunion: Eros and Psyche; the dreamer and the watcher.

What's essential is the idea of reunion; there has been provided, in reality, an exact replica of dream. Which event presumably erases the need for compensation or escape. And yet two primary responses suggest themselves: one can repudiate the translation or, in a kind of exorcism, one may permit the actual to supplant the dreamed. But immersion in time is a shock, involving real forfeits—of perfection, of the fantasy of eternity. That shock could be predicted. The surprise is that there are benefits to this perspective. To someone who feels, however briefly, without longing or regret, life on the shore, the life of dream, of waiting, seems suddenly tragic in its implications.

"Mild expectancy": what can be wrong with that? The lover hardly seems to be suffering. In his fatigue, he relaxes easily into the natural cycle, whereas the speaker's conscious determination places her outside these rhythms. This determination to stay awake is fueled by terror; it is, throughout the poem, a continuous, an active, choice. Expectancy, the sign of a heart set on the future—suddenly this seems a grave misuse of time. To dream, to yearn, or, in the realm of consciousness, to plan, to calculate—all a waste, a delusion. To live this way is to slight the earth. Not that the future isn't *real*. The delusion lies in projecting oneself into it indefinitely. One cannot live both there and here.

What the future holds is clear enough: the beach, the night world are dense with presentiments. Everywhere is stillness, the stillness of sleep which cannot help but resemble the stillness of death. What life there is regresses, the gulls, by example, transformed into clusters of cells. This is a warning, the message being: time is short. I hope a reader senses, in the poem's slow unreeling, interrupted with recurring commands, the degree to which this speaker is subject to the lure of the regressive. Her urgency reflects her own desire to capitulate and, in this sense, she sings to herself to keep awake, like someone on a vigil, a firewatch. There is, to put it plainly, an aspect of this which is pure pep talk.

The worst this poem can imagine is "what happens to the dreamers." The worst is to sleep through a life. By definition, it doesn't matter what the lover dreams; if he dreams, he isn't watching. Nor has the speaker's "weakness" been cured forever. Forever is, in itself, the dreamer's word. As for the peace passion gives: it could be called courage. Among the residual gifts of love is a composure, an openness to all experience, so profound it amounts to an acceptance of death. Or, more accurately, the future is no longer necessary. One is not rash, neither is one paralyzed by conservatism or hope. Simply, the sense of having lived, of having known one's fate, is very strong. And that sensation tells us what it is to live without the restrictions of fear. Such moments, in a way, have nothing to teach; they can be neither contrived nor prolonged by will. What they establish is a standard. Not forever, but for once it was possible to refuse consolation, to refuse the blindfold.

"Night Song" issues from, is made possible by, a sudden confidence. Whether finally or briefly, the soul can expose itself to "the revolutions," the massive cycles and upheavals of time. This is the greatest freedom we can know; its source, in the poem, is love, but the experience itself, the sense of being no longer "compelled," is an experience of autonomy. The lover's alert presence is necessary to confirm these sensations, since such experiences must be tested, witnessed.

What the speaker wants is *presence,* not union, dissolution, but the condition which preceded it. The choice is not between dreaming and lovemaking (another escape of self) but between dreaming and watching. Simultaneous consciousness, in other words—the exultant recognition of one soul by another. The ideal of balance has replaced the fantasy of incorporation. Contact of this sort seems to exist outside of time, beyond the laws of earth: all motion, whether toward fusion or separation, ends it. Motion is the first law. And as surely as the speaker's state dramatizes one of the soul's primary aims—to exist distinctly, to know where it ends and the blur of the world begins—so will the conflicting aim be asserted as the wish to dissolve, to be allied with, absorbed into another. The drive toward oblivion seems to me (as to many others) not a symptom of sickness but a true goal, and this wish of the self to do away with the very boundaries it has struggled to discover and maintain seems to me an endless subject, however we may try to subvert its grandeur.

I don't think of "Night Song" as a love poem. Love is a stimulus, and the advantage of writing out of situations of this kind seems to me an advantage of subject and attitude: one can write as lovers speak, of what is crucial in simple language.

The underlying subject seems to me to be individuality, without which no love can exist—groups do not love other groups. Love connects one irreplaceable being to another: the payment is terror of death, since if each person is unique, each death is singular, an eternal isolation. That we have common drives is consoling, but to dwell on them is to evade the issue of ultimate solitude. The relationships, in this poem, of the various forms of oblivion, of dream to orgasm to death, are less important than the perception of oblivion, in any form, as noncollective. If the pronouns in the last line are changed to "we" and "our," the line is instantly cloying, conventional; the sentiment thus expressed is paraphrased many times in the archives of Hallmark. Even if the second person is retained and only the possessive deleted, the thought turns vague—that in the second instance the line is also destroyed as a rhythmic unit is another problem. "You'll get oblivion"; "We'll get our oblivion": despite extreme discrepancies of tone, both sentences express the idea that oblivion is an alternative to self. Total eradication or complete union. "Night Song" suggests that the oblivion we ultimately achieve is an outpost of solitude from which the other is exiled—your oblivion is not mine, as your dream is not. This last line makes a mockery of placation; it damns the wish it grants. Against the relentless pronoun, the verbs are drumbeats, infantile, primitive. If what we want is oblivion, we are all lucky.

A last point. We are given to assume that morality depends on a regard for consequences. To some extent, this is surely true. But the regard is felt as fear—in this light, morality appears a product of intimidation. If "Night Song" connects the idea of freedom to rejection of the future, what is diminished, emotionally, is greed. Not avidity, but compulsive acquisition, need projected into time, the self straining to predict and provide for all foreseeable deficiency. I think the word *free* has no meaning if it does not suggest freedom from greed. To live in the present must mean being unerringly decisive, but choice, there, is easier, not harder. I do not claim to live at this plane, but I can imagine it.

It was clear to me long ago that any hope I had of writing real poetry depended on my living through common experiences. The privileged, the too-protected, the mandarin in my nature would have to be checked. At the same time, I was wary of drama, of disaster too deliberately courted: I have always been too at ease with extremes. What had to be cultivated, beyond a necessary neutrality, was the willingness to be identified with others. Not with the single other, the elect, but with a human community. My wish was to be special. But the representative life I wanted to record had somehow to be lived.

Major experiences vary in form—what reader and writer learn to do is recognize analogies. I watched my house burn—in the category of major losses, this made only the most modest start. Nor was it unexpected: I had spent twenty years waiting to undergo the losses I knew to be inevitable. I was obsessed with loss; not surprisingly, I was also acquisitive, possessive. The two tendencies fed each other; every impulse to extend my holdings increased the fundamental anxiety. Actual loss, loss of mere property, was a release, an abrupt transition from anticipation to expertise. In passing, I learned something about fire, about its appetite. I watched the destruction of all that had been, all that would not be again, and all that remained took on a radiance.

These are, in the deepest sense, ordinary experiences. On the subject of change, of loss, we all attain to authority. In my case, the timing was efficient. I was in my late thirties; perhaps I'd learned all I could about preparation, about gathering. The next lesson is abandon, letting go.

Perhaps, too, in all this there were other messages to be heard. And perhaps ''Night Song'' sounds much more of a piece with my other work than this suggests. It wouldn't surprise me. It seems these are the messages I'm equipped to receive.

JORIE GRAHAM

Two Paintings by Gustav Klimt

Although what glitters
    on the trees,
row after perfect row,
    is merely
the injustice
    of the world,

the chips on the bark of each
    beech tree
catching the light, the sum
    of these delays
is the beautiful, the human
    beautiful,

body of flaws.
    The dead
would give anything,
    I'm sure,
to step again onto
    the leafrot,

into the avenue of mottled shadows,
    the speckled,
broken skins. The dead
    in their sheer
open parenthesis, what they
    wouldn't give

for something to lean on
    that won't
give way. I think I
    would weep

for the moral nature
    of this world,

for right and wrong like pools
    of shadow
and light you can step in
    and out of
crossing this yellow beech forest,
    this *buchen-wald*,

one autumn afternoon, late
    in the twentieth
century, in hollow light,
    in gaseous light . . .
To receive the light
    and return it

and stand in rows, anonymous,
    is a sweet secret
even the air wishes
    it could unlock.
See how it pokes at them
    in little hooks,

the blue air, the yellow trees.
    Why be afraid?
They say when Klimt
    died suddenly
a painting, still
    incomplete,

was found in his studio,
    a woman's body
open at its point of
    entry,
rendered in graphic,
    pornographic,

detail—something like
    a scream
between her legs. Slowly,
    feathery,
he had begun to paint
    a delicate

garment (his trademark)
    over this mouth
of her body. The mouth
    of her face
is genteel, bored, feigning a need
    for sleep. The fabric

defines the surface,
    the story,
so we are drawn to it,
    its blues
and yellows glittering
    like a stand

of beech trees late
    one afternoon
in Germany, in fall.
    It is called
Buchenwald, it is
    1890. In

the finished painting
    the argument
has something to do
    with pleasure.

Pleasure

"Klimt" began on a day in Arcata, after a long rain, the sun suddenly blazing every wet thing. I was in a friend's small apartment overlooking her garden. Outside, row after row of ripe tomatoes, lettuces, squash, gleamed. And, nearer to us, contained by a crisp wire mesh, a compost heap, open at the top. We could see the layers of refuse through the chicken wire. What astonished me most of all, I recall, leaning against the glass pane looking out (my friend and I had just had a fight and were silent) was how all the birds, all the bright ones, the ones with clever sharp-edged beaks, were at the compost heap, taking turns. No one would have seen them or stopped them among the fat vegetables and fruit. No one would have cared because no one was watching. But they took their turns—a hierarchy made itself legible soon enough—over and under and through the mesh restraint. I cannot say how clean the air seemed: it almost hurt me to have to look through it into the world of things. And the silence in our room seemed made only for us to look out, pressing outward, into what seemed to be a world of urgent and hungry clues. What did they say? Inside, on the wall, on a large glossy calendar I saw a painting of a beech forest (in the same kind of light) by Gustav Klimt. I noticed the words *buchen-wald* meant beech forest in German. Later that evening I read in a book on Gustav Klimt the story about the painting found after his death, unfinished, in the studio. He had gone for a walk, if I recall correctly, and suffered a heart attack.

One day, a month or so later, as decay began to set into the summer, and again after a great rain and sudden sunlight out of nowhere, I took a walk. I took my tiny hand-held tape recorder along. During a three-hour walk all the way through town, down to the abandoned pier, up the graveyard, through the main square, and back, the whole first draft came. I know I have a poem if I am moved in the first draft. By moved I mean choking in spots. If I don't have this feeling I throw it away. I have, in the past, wasted months on work that began with an idea, an idea alone. Now I know, for myself at least, to let go at that point. If the first draft isn't nerved by an emotion I didn't know I felt, it isn't going to be governed by any ideas I didn't already understand before I wrote the poem. I always think of Frost saying, "no surprise for the writer, no surprise for the reader." He adds, of course, "no tears for the writer, no tears for the reader." There can be something like tears blazing all over notions; ideas are vastly and deeply part of the body. A good idea seizes the whole machine. A new idea makes you physically afraid, your body changes. Hope is lodged in your skin, in your cellwork. I cannot even begin to understand the division commonly drawn (and honestly experienced by many people) between thought and emotion.

Possibly the steps, the rhythm, of a walking motion have influenced the breath lengths and line lengths in this poem, and other poems I have written in this form. I remember—perhaps it is a myth, but a useful one to me—hearing that Yeats composed while walking. Mandelstam writes, about Dante, how he can tell from the measure of the language that the lines were written while walking. Perhaps this is nonsense. But there is something about being the stillness in another, perpetually moving world which imitates, for me at least (or is it *mimics?*), an illusion of eternity in the midst of flux. This is easy to see. Sitting at a desk, or in a room where nothing moves, you become the relative motion. Outside, watching everything fall away while you stay, you transform the visible into the invisible inner world; outside, among all those failures of the visible, the inner world may be experienced as the center, the government. It makes me feel my soul is an eye or an ear. And the tape recorder (with its clicks indicating line breaks) imitates this careful probing very accurately. Somehow the outer world, with its incredibly unquestionable thereness, makes me justify my words in its

midst as I move through it. It is harder to speak something
untrue, dishonest, phony, or merely invented for the pur-
poses of a poem, in the face of trees and power lines and other
people's faces and evidence of joblessness and the damage
done by the most recent rains. And then, too, I experience my
work in the midst of their work, and must be honest not to
feel ashamed. And my hurrying in the midst of theirs. This is
difficult to speak about, but walking through neighborhoods
where the very real work of daily choosing and suffering is al-
ways continuing, it is harder to speak junk, or write lies
down. And then, too, I hear myself say it out loud long before
I see it on the page. And I can feel my own embarrassment
(even if I'm whispering) if I'm posturing or playing at feeling.
I don't do this too often, although many of the poems in *Ero-
sion* came this way.

This is not unlike the way fact operates when placed in the
midst of a poem. I think of Yeats's stone in the stream
("Easter 1916"). I remember reading not long ago about the
man, in California I believe, who offered a large sum of
money to the person who could prove the Holocaust really oc-
curred. This frightened me a good deal, but why? A court case
ensued. Vast amounts of records and photographs were
brought in. Testimony from survivors. An endless flow on the
witness stand. Eventually the judge decided there was suffi-
cient (although it seems not overwhelming) evidence. A good
deal of what we bank on as fact had been deemed insufficient,
spurious, irrelevant, unprovable, hearsay, etc. And I think
how now, with the new technology, photographs can be
made and unmade by computers. Whole faces lifted, altered,
and returned. The work is done on the negative. But isn't this
the very work of adjectives? I ask myself. Hasn't this always
been so? Why does it frighten me so to feel the bedrock
slipping, the greater arbiter of our conduct, the *thereness* of
things, of some facts at least, facts from whose stare we can-
not hide claiming increasingly subjective "versions" of reali-
ty's "text"? Because, it seems to me, in doing so we finally
end up letting ourselves off the hook; if it is not *there*, finally,
and *knowable*, finally, how can we be responsible for it, to it,

split atom or pool of blood? And so I try to bring fact into a
poem for my own good, in order to experience the limits of
the imagination, if you will, in order to feel (in the act of writ-
ing the poem) what it is that escapes me, what judges me,
keeping me true.

What I am saying is that speaking something that is true
and discovering something more deeply true than what you
already know is important to me. And so I proceed, by the
short lines, with a kind of slowed sternness, a caution of
thought and emotion—or, more than a caution, a fearful care;
I think of the pace of these short lines as the pace of a mind
thinking as if everything depended on its accuracy, the sen-
tences deliberately slowed to make one feel *You cannot undo
what you say.* . . . I think of the pace of religious music, the
speed at which you walk through a large cathedral. The pace
at which you look at a great painting on the wall of that cathe-
dral. All the silence around them, I hope, makes the words
feel *wrought from* their alternatives. This is always the case in
poems, I know, but here I wanted to make it part of the sub-
ject, and so I exaggerated, negotiating more actively with si-
lence on the page than I have before. I imagine the line
breaks—even in their strangeness—impart the feeling of deep
control to the reader as he or she proceeds. Not control of the
will as much as the control the heart feels moving through
depths, moving *in,* as much brave as afraid. Because it *is* fear-
ful, what there is to be found out. At least as much as it is joy-
ful. . . .

Just as here, in this poem, going under the fabric, the dress
each soul wears—garments which become the surface, the
whole visible world—you find the scream; beneath one name
for *Buchen-wald* you find the other name, beneath the most
honest love you find the terror. . . . And the poem I hope,
enacts the movement from one to the other. Hopefully one
discovers, feeling one's way through, that they are not sepa-
rate, the love and the violence, that they are the same, and
that only our choice—not our natures—keeps us on one side
or the other. It is frightening to come to know this about one-

self. And intoxicating, to me, that poems can enact this, that the writing of the poem can teach you, the writer, this. Because those poems that move me are enactments of discovery, not retellings. In those poems that change me the speaker is most often the protagonist, not the narrator. The narrator knows he will survive the poem. The protagonist never knows if he will even make it to the end; the poem itself becomes the act of survival, the act of flailing and probing, an open desire for grace or change. I think this is what Stevens meant when he said the poem is the *act* of the mind in the process of finding what will suffice. Not having found what will. . . .

And so here, in this case, my action surprised me, changed me, as follows: I wrote the poem originally from the perspective of the woman. The woman whose vagina was painted by the titillated old man, whose body was then further violated by its being covered up with mere ornament. I felt anger at the story, and that anger came through, as well, as anger at all such dehumanizations, at the Buchenwald under the mere beech forest (at the trick of language, of fabric, of pigment . . .), at the anonymous layered dead of history. It took me a long while to realize I had to write the poem, as well, from the perspective of the painter. That the act of writing the poem in and of itself made me his ally. That my humanity made me his accomplice. And the accomplice of all victimizers, by implication, not just the victims. That the desire to transform makes us all, by extension, and potentially, murderers. That it is, again, our choice not our nature that divides us. And that it is our circumstance probably more than our choice, finally, that saves us from becoming our enemies . . . our place in time, our wading through the forest in 1890 rather than 1940. I worry in political poems about the us/them divisions often being drawn. Are we not capable of the same atrocity? Have you not felt it in your soul, your fingertips? It worries me because although it might be the purpose of journalism, political theory, even philosophy, to help us take sides, make choices, I think it is the most important function of poetry to make the writer (and the reader) feel his or her humanity more deeply, his or her kinship. Not only with the portions of humanity it is easy to see one's kinship with, but also with those one too easily denies responsibility for, the portions one secretly congratulates oneself for being unlike. Often I'll assign a poem like Forché's nonetheless remarkable "The Colonel," for instance, and ask the students to write it over from the colonel's point of view (so that the relative, deeply buried self-implication and the absolute blame are reversed). This does not, obviously, make for a "better" poem, only for a better understanding of what poetry is. If that is not in our poems, if that is not in our hearts, if we don't know how deeply and easily we can be him, in fact *are* him often, daily, then poetry has failed its most precious function. . . .

I think of how profoundly James Wright knew, enacted, and reenacted this—in his Doty poems, for example. He never flattered himself, never let himself, or us, off the hook. And so, in this case, this poem, it is both of our *pleasures* I must admit to at the end: the more bitter, ironic tone carries one *pleasure,* the pleasure of anger, the fury at being worked upon by this man's hands and art; and then the other *pleasure* (and its tone is exhausted, sad), equally true and equally human, the pleasure of doing what he has done, of having too much power, of being giddy with it, the fire in your hands, and creating and stealing and, in effect, murdering. It horrified me when I realized this was true. It is taking me years to understand Jon Anderson's remarkable lines:

I believe in the mirror, its terrible empty reflection,
in the progress from judgement towards compassion.

DONALD HALL

The Black Faced Sheep

Ruminant pillows! Gregarious soft boulders!

If one of you found a gap in a stone wall,
the rest of you—rams, ewes, bucks, wethers, lambs;
mothers and daughters, old grandfather-father,
cousins and aunts, small bleating sons—
followed onward, stupid
as sheep, wherever
your leader's sheep-brain wandered to.

My grandfather spent all day searching the valley
and edges of Ragged Mountain,
calling "Ke-*day!*" as if he brought you salt,
"Ke-*day!* Ke-*day!*"

* * *

When the shirt wore out, and darns in the woolen
shirt needed darning,
a woman in a white collar
cut the shirt into strips and braided it,
as she braided her hair every morning.

In a hundred years
the knees of her great-granddaughter
crawled on a rug made from the wool of sheep
whose bones were mud,
like the bones of the woman, who stares
from an oval in the parlor.

* * *

I forked the brambly hay down to you
in nineteen-fifty. I delved my hands deep
in the winter grass of your hair.

When the shearer cut to your nakedness in April
and you dropped black eyes in shame,
hiding in barnyard corners, unable to hide,
I brought grain to raise your spirits,
and ten thousand years
wound us through pasture and hayfield together,
threads of us woven
together, three hundred generations
from Africa's hills to New Hampshire's.

*   *   *

You were not shrewd like the pig.
You were not strong like the horse.
You were not brave like the rooster.

Yet none of the others looked like a lump of granite
that grew hair,
and none of the others
carried white fleece as soft as dandelion seed
around a black face,
and none of them sang such a flat and sociable song.

*   *   *

Now the black faced sheep have wandered and will not return,
though I search the valleys
and call "Ke-*day*" as if I brought them salt.

Now the railroad draws
a line of rust through the valley. Birch, pine, and maple
lean from cellarholes
and cover the dead pastures of Ragged Mountain
except where machines make snow
and cables pull money up hill, to slide back down.

* * *

At South Danbury Church twelve of us sit—
cousins and aunts, sons—
where the great-grandfathers of the forty-acre farms
filled every pew.
I look out the window at summer places,
at Boston lawyers' houses
with swimming pools cunningly added to cowsheds,
and we read an old poem aloud, about Israel's sheep
—and I remember faces and wandering hearts,
dear lumps of wool—and we read

that the rich farmer, though he names his farm for himself,
takes nothing into his grave;
that even if people praise us, because we are successful,
we will go under the ground
to meet our ancestors collected there in the darkness;
that we are all of us sheep, and death is our shepherd,
and we die as the animals die.

Notes on
''The Black Faced Sheep''

1. Poems begin when something in the present—event or object, word overheard—calls power to itself by association with something alive in the mind's recesses, some connection potent but unavailable to consciousness. Images and sounds fill the space between the visible present and the source I remain unaware of. Sometimes in the long process of composition I become aware of what was hidden. Years later, sometimes I discover something further.

2. Ten years ago I bought an etching by Henry Moore. His gallery sent me a catalog announcing a portfolio of sheep drawings, and the cover reproduced the head of a black faced sheep with wonderful eyes. I wrote Moore (many years ago I did a book about him) and bought the etching, framed it, set it in the living room, and started gazing at it. It's a sheepy sheep: you can smell it, its squiggly hair is oily with lanolin— yet it creates in itself an ennobling distance; it's nobody's *trompe l'oeil.* Staring at it daily, I went dreamy with it; I wanted to hum its tune or read it or do any number of things inappropriate to an etching. . . . I recognized the approaches of a poem.

It used to be that a poem did not *approach.* A poem arrived full-grown and unfinished, wearing a suit of chicken feathers and aluminum, jumping about, clawing the furniture and leaving green spots on the rug. Now, as befits the ponderosity of late-middle years, poems *approach,* on leaden feet. Eight years ago I recognized the approaches of a poem because the etching tranced me into associations, and because associated phrases and words (not a whole poem-draft) began to turn up in my notebook. I kept a folder for slips of paper that pointed toward a black faced sheep. . . .

Gradually I understood that I was not obsessed with an etching of a Suffolk cross that a Yorkshire sculptor had observed on rolling Hertfordshire land. The images that followed each other, the words that gathered in shapeless clumps on the page derived from summers on a New Hampshire farm where my grandfather had tended a herd of fifty sheep. The recollections were pleasant: except for birthing and shearing, except for ticks and dogs and illness, sheep are not so much work as cattle, nor so demanding as pigs or chickens. They spend the summer cheerfully untended, cropping bushy pasture grass and drinking from any puddle or brook, needing little except for salt every now and then. In the barns of winter they need daily feeding, but they will eat brambly hay that cows sniff at. . . .

But I talk about sheep instead of a sheep-poem. I had known these creatures in company with my grandfather, and when I remembered the sheep—I am sure when I began staring at Moore's etching—I remembered my grandfather. I loved to hear him talk as he milked the cows or as the horse plodded us back from haying or as we hiked to salt the sheep. He told me stories, recited poems, wrapped me in anecdotes from a rich life. I cherished his words, loved him, and learned from him as I have done with few men.

Much later it occurred to me that another such man was Henry Moore, not old enough to be my grandfather but thirty years older than I am. Of great importance to me, Moore has been a model, more than any of the poets I have known, of dedication to an art combined with brains, humor, and decency. And as I began working on the poem in Ann Arbor in 1974, I knew that I would buy the farm when my grandmother died; I knew that Jane and I would soon leave to spend a year there; maybe I knew that once we went there, we would never come back; I knew that I would spend all day writing as Moore spent all day working at sculpture and graphics—something for which I had envied him over twenty years.

I would go to the farm, to take my grandfather's place and to live like Henry Moore. It was the sheep that allowed me to bring the men together.

3. As I wrote the poem, material accumulated at a great rate, arriving in the longish line that I had found a year earlier in "Kicking the Leaves." Lines and anecdotes and scenes entered my notebook; the subject dragged its net in the sea and caught sheep-fish. . . . I heard my grandfather call them: *ke-day, ke-day, ke-day;* I saw them in the fields. Working over my lines daily, finding new associations, cutting and refining, the months went by.

I left Ann Arbor pulling a U-Haul. Writing again, I found the many pages of notes diminishing, a sequence in long sections shortening, becoming more nearly a single thing. Then one Sunday at the church down the road in New Hampshire, the responsive reading was Psalm 49, which is a song of despair and hell, of failure and decay softened only by the knowledge that everyone comes to the same end. Because I lamented the necessary passing of the old world, because I was guilty for my temporary replacement of my grandparents, because Henry Moore was almost eighty, the psalm filled me as wind fills a sail.

> . . .Wise men die;
> The fool and the brutish alike perish
> And leave their wealth to others.
> Their inward thought is that their house shall continue
>   forever . . .
> They call their lands their own names.
> But man . . . abideth not:
> He is like the beasts that perisheth.

And men are not like *any* beast; they resemble the one animal that grazes through both the Old and the New Testament:

> They are appointed as a flock for Sheol;
> Death shall be their shepherd.

4. There are times when everything you look at blooms with metaphor, when the world is a code embodying your feelings, when the graffito echoes your thought and the birdsong assorts itself to your mood. As I look at Psalm 49 years later, it startles me how *little* the psalm had to do with the poem, how I wrenched and devoured it for my purpose. . . .

Things come together—or they seem to, which is enough. If I am patient, if I stay with a poem, things will come together. . . . "The Black Faced Sheep" took between two and three years, more than a hundred drafts.

Lately, poems have not been coming so quickly.

ROBERT HASS

The Harbor at Seattle

They used to meet one night a week at a place on top of Telegraph Hill to explicate Pound's *Cantos*—Peter who was a scholar; and Linda who could recite many of the parts of the poem that envisioned paradise; and Bob who wanted to understand the energy and surprise of its music; and Bill who knew Greek and could tell them that "Dioce, whose terraces were the color of stars" was a city in Asia Minor mentioned by Herodotus.

And that winter when Bill locked his front door and shot himself in the heart, the others remembered the summer nights, after a long session of work, when they would climb down the steep stairs which negotiated the cliff where the hill faced the waterfront to go somewhere to get a drink and talk. The city was all lights at that hour and the air smelled of coffee and the bay.

In San Francisco coffee is a family business, and a profitable one, so the members of the families are often on the society page of the newspaper, which is why Linda remembered the wife of one of the great coffee merchants who had also killed herself; it was a memory from childhood, from those first glimpses a newspaper gives of the shape of the adult world, and it mixed now with the memory of the odor of coffee and the salt air.

And Peter recalled that the museum had a photograph of that woman by Minor White. They had all seen it. She had bobbed hair and a smart suit on with sharp lapels and padded shoulders, and her skin was perfectly clear. Looking directly into the camera, she does not seem happy but she seems confident; and it is as if Minor White understood that her elegance,

because it was a matter of style, was historical, because be-
hind her is an old barn which is the real subject of the
picture—the grain of its wood planking so sharply focussed
that it seems alive, greys and blacks in a rivery and complex
pattern of venation.

The back of Telegraph Hill was not always so steep. At the
time of the earthquake, building materials were scarce, so
coastal ships made a good thing of hauling lumber down from
the northwest. But the economy was paralyzed, there were
no goods to take back north, so they dynamited the side of the
hill and used the blasted rock for ballast, and then, in port
again, they dumped the rock in the water to take on more
lumber, and that was how they built the harbor in Seattle.

Images

Just down from the mountains, early August. Lugging my youngest child from the car, I noticed that his perfectly relaxed body was getting heavier every year. When I undressed him, he woke up enough to mumble, "I like my own bed," then fell back down, all the way down, into sleep. The sensation of his weight was still in my arms as I shut the door.

In our bed, in a bundled, parti-colored mass of light, grandmother's quilt, our eldest son. Aspirin on the dresser beside the bed, Kleenex, pencils, Nicolaides's *The Natural Way to Draw*, Kerouac's *The Dharma Bums*. Twenty years old, home from college, in love, working construction, he gets a summer cold and in our absence climbs into our bed to nurse himself.

The kitchen, with that mix of familiarity and strangeness absence gives a room, is clean and smells strongly of bruised apples still simmering from the afternoon heat. On the table, a note in the large open hand of my daughter. "Sweethearts, I've gone to work! Muffins in the drawer, coffee in the fridge. Pick me up at four." She graduated from high school in June. Evidently she had friends over last night, got up earlier than they to go to her job at the merry-go-round in the park. In the cleanliness of the kitchen, the large freedom of her hand, even the choice of a red pen, are written a kind of independence and command, a new delicious pleasure in herself. High school seniors, a friend remarked, are older than college freshmen.

The moon is just rising at midnight. It is past half, a swollen egg, and floods the rooms with light. I walk around checking. Everything seems alright. Outside on the deck where they have been spread to dry, beach towels in the moonlight.

"If the Spectator," Blake wrote, "could enter into these Images in his Imagination, approaching them on the Fiery Chariot of his Contemplative Thought . . . or could make a

Friend & Companion of one of these Images of wonder . . .
then would he arise from his Grave, then would he meet the
Lord in the Air & then would he be happy." And Eliot wrote:

> I am moved by fancies that are curled
> Around these images and cling

Last summer I had written about beach towels drying on a
fence in the early morning heat. I think it pleased me as much
as anything I wrote last year, but I knew that it had seemed
slight to everyone who saw it. I had somehow not gotten it
right. If this were the seventeenth century, Japan, if I were
Kikaku or Rensetsu, I would have gone to Basho, the master,
and said, "How about this? Beach towels drying in the moon-
light." And Basho would have said, "Hass, you have Edo-
taste. You have the weakness of trying to say something
unusual. 'Beachtowels drying on a fence' is perhaps not good
enough. 'Beach towels drying in the moonlight' is bad, even if
it seems better at first, like one of those trees that flowers but
bears no fruit." Ten years or more they spent together, trying
to understand how to make an image.

In our room, our son having been dislodged tactfully from
the bed, my wife in the lamplight is rubbing lotion into her
skin and examining mosquito bites. That morning we had
been lying on warm granite beside a lake the melting snow
fed, and her breasts are a little sunburned.

We had driven down late in an old car with a new transmis-
sion that made shifting difficult. Cool air, then the flat heat of
the central valley, the traffic moving in fluid patterns like
schooling fish. In bed the freedom and coolness of the sheets
is one very good thing and the pouring out of those images
that night driving suppresses is another. Languorous, halluci-
natory, they may be the best thing about summer.

Gradually, I pick one out. We are in camp in the morning.
Cleaning up after breakfast, talking. I am fiddling with a
Coleman lantern. One of our friends is remembering a time,
at eighteen or nineteen, when she began to develop a repeti-
tion compulsion. Its rituals—handwashing, rechecking pilot
lights, performing tasks and then obsessively performing

them again—were invading her life and she was terrified. Her parents, so embarrassed by the idea of mental illness that they could not bring themselves to speak of it, finally arranged for her to see a psychiatrist contacted by her father through the health insurance officer of the company he worked for. A stone building downtown, frosted doors, tile floors, walnut paneling.

Telling us this, she is rapt, alive to the memory. She has a skillet in one hand, a scouring pad in the other. Both hang limply at her sides for a moment while she considers. We are camped on a granite shelf in the saddle of a canyon. Silver Creek runs past our camp and one can see it glinting and leaping down the long valley to a meadow in the distance where it joins the east fork of the Carson River. High walls of granite on either side, ridges of cypress and pine, snow-patches, an immense blue sky. Just above her on a cedar limb a Steller's jay is eyeing the grains of cooked millet she has scraped onto the ground.

"I asked him, I told him what was happening and said there was just one thing I wanted to know and that was, was I ever going to get over this? and he said, probably not." Suddenly she burst into tears. The occasion of the story was parents; another friend, shaking out a sleeping bag, began to talk about her mother, how when she was about to leave a marriage of twenty years, her mother had called her to say that she was coldhearted for not responding to the fact that the younger sister, the darling of the family, had lost her suitcase while traveling in Europe. She had not at first seen her friend's tears, and she trailed off now, her milder grievance suspended. The first woman was sitting on the ground, sobbing, her shoulders shaking. The man she was with came up and put a hand on her shoulder. My son, who had been assiduously practicing a card trick someone had taught him the night before and half-listening to the conversation, flicked me a quick look. Was this good sadness or bad sadness? And then went back to his cards.

The woman on the ground, forty years old now, long past that terror, stopped crying, took a couple of deep breaths, sighed, got up, and began to clean the pan again. "The thing is, I guess, he was right in a way. I don't suppose we ever get over anything." The jay had lit on the ground at a safe distance, still eyeing the millet. Someone else said, "Yeah. A healed bone hurts in the winter." My son looked to his mother this time, to see, I think, if she regarded this proposition as true. Resumptions are a curious spectacle. The boy friend now felt rather wooden with his hand protectively on his lover's shoulder. He gave her an awkward hug. The other friend, embarrassed at not having caught the woman's tone, made a connection that had not quite been there between the two stories. It was the social equivalent of parting one's hair at the ear to camouflage baldness. No one is deceived, it looks peculiar, but it is an acceptable convention.

In stories, in incidents that might be stories, I suppose there is always a moment, different for different memories, when the image, the set of relationships that seem actually to reveal something about life, forms. Lying in bed, what came to me all in one swiftness was the forty-year-old woman, lithe-bodied, with the beginnings of hard lines around the eyes and mouth, in the morning light, in dusty thermal underwear, with a pan and a scouring pad hanging slackly in her hands and the startled, becalmed, remembering look on her face, just before the access of grief; and the jay in the tree above the white millet grains scattered among brown pine needles; and the oblivious friend telling her story; and the alert small boy practicing a card trick; and the long moraine of glacier-smooth granite behind them that the river traversed and the green meadow in the far distance, with just a foam of white wild-flowers flecking it; and me, I suppose, the watcher fiddling with his lantern.

It has always seemed to me that if one could get those moments, and get them faithfully, one might come close to grasping the fabled monster, being. The sort of image one would produce then would be not quite an idea, stiller than that, with less implication outside itself; more a thought than an idea. And it would not be a myth, it wouldn't have that explanatory power; it would be more like pure story. Nor would it be a metaphor; it would not say this is that, it would say this is. Metonymy rather than a metaphor, the part standing for the whole from the belief that any part of the world, seen absolutely, is the world. Roland Barthes, in *The Empire of Signs*, says that Japanese poems are about nothing, pure signifiers without the hawk's swoop of signification, because they signify only themselves. He quotes by way of evidence a poem by Basho:

> How admirable!
> to see lightning and not think
> life is fleeting

Which is not itself an example. But the point is clear enough: to *see* lightning. "The Harbor at Seattle," whatever its success, was written in this spirit. Its elements had been rattling around in my head, the story about Telegraph Hill, the group who met on that hill in a city to study Pound's poem which is full of the magic of cities, the Minor White photograph, the smell of roasting coffee, the suicide of my friend. And when they assembled themselves in a shape, I wanted to render that form as faithfully as possible, which is why, I think, it came to be written in a prose which I like to think has some resemblance to *haibun*, to the haiku-like prose of the Japanese poets.

Chekhov recorded this in his notebook: "They were mineral water bottles with preserved cherries in them." The context lost—is a mineral water bottle the equivalent of a Coke bottle? What sort of diligence, refinement, husbandry do the preserved cherries imply?—it still gives a small, intense thrill of pleasure. Perhaps the very loss of context, like the lost context of the animals drawn on the walls of the Lascaux caves, intensifies it. What we see clearly is not perhaps being toward which the image leaps, but the quiet attention which is the form of that impulse to leap. Here are some other entries from his notebook:

A bedroom. The light of the moon shines so brightly through the window that even the buttons on his nightshirt are visible.

They undressed the corpse but had no time to take off the gloves; a corpse in gloves.

In July the red bird sings the whole morning.

Prostitutes in Monte Carlo, the whole tone of the place. The palm trees, it seems, are prostitutes, and the chickens are prostitutes.

An actress who spoilt all her parts by very bad acting— and this continued all her life long until she died. Nobody liked her; she ruined all the best parts; and yet she went on acting until she was seventy.

He got a bronze medal for the census of 1897.

A clever fresh sensible girl. When she bathed, he noticed her ribcage, her skinny behind. He got to hate her.

This is very close to the temperament of Japanese poets. Here is one by Issa:

> The man pulling radishes
> pointed my way
> with a radish.

And, from the opposite point of view, by Buson:

> Digging in the field—
> the man who asked the way
> has disappeared.

January 16 was a holiday in the Japan of the Tokugawa Shogunate. Apprentices who had been sent from home to learn a trade were given a day off to visit their families. The day also had associations with kite flying. Buson gives us one kid on the way home:

          Apprentice's holiday:
        hops over kite string,
          keeps going.

That easy leap is like William Carlos Williams, but it is when
you start thinking about the kite tugging in the wind that the
poem opens up. Often enough, when a thing is seen clearly,
there is a sense of absence about it—it is true of impressionist
painting—as if the more palpable it is, the more some im-
mense subterranean displacement seems to be working in it,
as if at the point of truest observation the visible and invisible
exerted terrific counterpressure. Some of Buson's poems
seem to comment on this directly:

          Mustard flowers,
        no whale in sight,
          the sea darkening.

   Images haunt. There is a whole mythology built on this fact;
Cezanne painting until his eyes bled, Wordsworth wandering
the Lake Country hills in an impassioned daze. Blake de-
scribes it very well, or Tu Fu's colleague who said to him: "It
is like being alive twice." In the nineteenth century, one
would have said that what compelled us was a sense of the
eternal. And it is something like that, some feeling in the ar-
rest of the image that what perishes and what lasts forever
have been brought into conjunction, and accompanying that
is a feeling of release from the self. Antonio Machado wrote:
"Hoy es siempre todavía." Now is always still. And Czeslaw
Milosz: *"Tylko trwa wieczna chwila."* Only the moment is eter-
nal. There is a delicate balance in this matter. Walking
through the rooms of my house on a moonlit August night,
with a sharp sense of my children each at a particular moment
in their lives and changing, with three or four shed, curled
leaves from a Benjamin fig on the floor of the dining room and
a spider, in that moonlight, already set to work in one of
them, and the dark outline of an old Monterey pine against
the sky outside the window, the one thing about the house
that seems never to have changed in the years of my living in

it, it is possible to feel my life, in a quiet ecstatic helplessness, as a long slow hurtle through the forms of things. I think I resist that sensation because there is a kind of passivity to it; I suppose that I fear it would make me careless of those things that need concentration to attend to.

But I would equally doubt its absence, which is what we usually mean by fact. The terror of facts is the purity of their arbitrariness. I live in this place, rather than that. Have this life, rather than that. It is August rather than September for physical and historical reasons too boring to go into and I am a man approaching middle age in the American century, which means I've had it easy, and I have three children, somewhere near the average, and I've just come home from summer vacation in an unreliable car. This is the *selva oscura*. Not that it isn't true, but that it is not the particular truth. It is the average, which is different from the common; arbitrary, the enemy of form. Moments exist by virtue of their velocity. They are eternal because they are gone in a second. This was the paradox Wallace Stevens had in mind when he wrote:

> Beauty is momentary in the mind,
>
> the fitful tracing of a portal,
> but in the flesh it is immortal.

It is this crossing of paths that the image seems to reconcile, and so it haunts us.

When Buson was dying in the winter of 1783, one of his friends reports, he spoke to his night nurse about the life of poetry. "Even being sick like this, my fondness for the way is beyond reason, and I try to make haiku. The high stage of *my dream hovers over the withered fields* is impossible for me to reach. Therefore, the old poet Basho's greatness is supremely moving to me now."* The poem he refers to is Basho's last,

*From Kito's "A Record of Buson's Last Days" in *Haiku Master Buson*, Yuki Sawa and Edith Shiffert (Heian International Publishing Co., 1978).

written when he was taken ill on a visit to Osaka in the fall of 1694. *"Tabi ni yamite yume wa kareno wo kakemeguru,"* it goes:

> Sick on a journey,
> my dream hovers
> over the withered fields.

Basho, late in his life, seems to have been torn between the way of religion and the way of art. He tried to stop writing poetry, he said, but was unable to do so, and he felt the choice as a kind of failure. He kept coming back to the search for the image. Some of his late poems have great serenity; all of them are solitary. This is one of the last, in R. H. Blyth's translation:

> Deep autumn,
> my neighbor, how
> does he live, I wonder?

Capable of enormous clarity, of an extraordinary emotional range, there is at the center of his work—as at the center of Rilke's or Baudelaire's—a sense of the sickness or incompleteness of existence. There is also a sense—rather like the sensation of driving when you lie in bed after a night of driving—of the unappeasable habit of the image. *Kareno*, in Basho's last poem, means "withered field." It is one of the conventional phrases of seasonal reference that almost all haiku contain. It identifies the time as late fall. Here it also means, I think, "the traditional seasonal phrase 'withered field.'" His dreams wander in the world and in the poem indistinguishably.

And it would seem wild with restlessness and grief, if it were not for the firmness of the syntax—and for something else that is a little difficult to describe. The phrase *yume wa*. *Yume* is dream or dreams, *wa* a particle indicating what's being talked about. One often sees it translated "as for." It is such a common feature of Japanese that to translate it at all is to begin to translate the culture rather than the language—and I don't know very much about either Japanese culture or the Japanese language. I have studied these poems without learning to speak Japanese, and I am afraid of a beginner's tendency to exaggerate differences. A literal translation might be "as for dream it hovers" or "wanders." I asked a Japanese friend if it would be closer to translate the phrase into English, "my dream wanders," or French, "le rêve s'égare." He shrugged hopelessly.

"There is no French word for dream, to me, that doesn't have the meaning of delusion. And all the words for wandering suggest error." He shook his head at the peculiarity of the French. "And everything in English has to be pinned down, your dream, my dream, and all the verbs are physical. *Yume wa,*" he made large circles with both hands, "means dream, the whole thing," more gestures, *"dream."*

Whatever the translation, it is that turn of phrase that gives the poem its deepest and most amazing effect. It is why the poem does not record sickness, yearning, unfulfillable hunger. Nor is it exactly objective or detached. It sits just in between, not detached but not attached either. Intense sadness and calm: nonattached, the Buddhists would say. It is an extraordinary act of consciousness that Buson was remembering in his dying master. It is also what any writer might say, not by way of avoidance but by way of explanation, when asked to comment on his own work: *as for dream, it wanders the withered fields.*

DONALD JUSTICE

Variations on Southern Themes

"But why do I write of the all unutterable and the all abysmal? Why does my pen not drop from my hand on approaching the infinite pity and tragedy of all the past? It does, poor helpless pen, with what it meets of the ineffable, what it meets of the cold Medusa-face of life, of all the life *lived*, on every side. *Basta, basta!*"

—H. James, *Notebooks*

1: At the Cemetery

Above the fence-flowers, like a bloody thumb,
A hummingbird was throbbing . . . And some
Petals had taken motion from the wings
In hardly observable obscure quiverings.
The mother stood there, but so still her clothing
Seemed to have settled into stone, nothing
To animate her face, nothing to read there—
O plastic rose O clouds O still cedar!
She stood there for a long time while the sky
Pondered her with its great Medusa-eye;
Or in the son's memory she did.

       And then a
Slow blacksnake, lazy with long sunning, slid
Down from its slab, and through the thick grass, and hid
Somewhere among the purpling wild verbena.

2: On the Farm

The boy, missing the city intensely at that moment,
Moped and sulked at the window. There went the first owl,
    quite near,
But the sound hardly registered. And the kerosene lamp
Went on sputtering, giving off vague medicinal fumes
That made him think of sickrooms. He had been memorizing
"The Ballad of Reading Gaol," but the lamplight hurt his
    eyes;
And he was too bored to sleep, restless and bored. *Years later,*
Perhaps, he would recall the evenings, empty and vast, when,
Under the first stars, there by the back gate, secretly, he
Had relieved himself on the shamed and drooping hollyhocks.
Now he yawned; the old dream of being a changeling re-
    turned.
And the owl cried, and he felt himself like the owl—proud,
    strange,
Almost invisible—or like some hero in Homer
Protected by the cloud let down by the gods to save him.

3:   In the Train,
Heading North through Florida,
Late at Night and Long Ago,
and Ending with a Line
from Thomas Wolfe

Midnight or after, and the little lights
Glittered like lost beads from a broken necklace
Beyond smudged windows, lost and irretrievable—
Some promise of romance those Southern nights
Never entirely kept—unless, sleepless,
We should pass down dim corridors again
To stand, braced in a swaying vestibule,
Alone with the darkness and the wind—out there
Nothing but pines and one new road perhaps,
Straight and white, aimed at the distant gulf—
And hear, from the smoking-room, the sudden high-pitched
Whinny of laughter pass from throat to throat;
And the great wheels smash and pound beneath our feet.

Notes on "Variations on Southern Themes"

It is true that there was a brief period, three or four years perhaps, when I thought of myself as a Southern writer. My first short story was anthologized in an O. Henry annual, and I was so carried away by the chance to make up a contributor's note that I found myself claiming to be "of the South" and with "no desire to leave it." The spell of Faulkner's wild and steamy prose was upon me in those days, and of the innocent fairy-tale world Eudora Welty's early stories conjured up. What they wrote seemed larger than life to me, an art of wonderful exaggerations and fantastications, a kind of dreaming; only dimly could anything like the South I had been born and brought up in be discerned beneath the mythic trappings. The ideas that gave me some purchase on this South, so much grander than my own, had come by way of the Fugitive-Agrarians. I wrote a master's thesis on their work, and for a while the sentimental ironies of their poetry imposed upon my own experience a set of attitudes which were not destined to survive.

A spoiled heroic figure like Faulkner's Sutpen had always been nearly as remote from my world, my desires and opinions, as Odysseus himself, and it should not have taken the hardening of Southern attitudes in the fifties—a reaction to the Supreme Court school decision—to drive home that realization finally. In poems of the time—"Beyond the Hunting Woods" and "Southern Gothic" in particular—I paid my respectful farewells to the symbols of the Old South, which seemed by then far more literary than lived. The decaying houses in those early poems represented the emptiness and hollowness I had come to find in such idealizations of the South, mixed, no doubt, with a certain lingering affection.

• • •

Driving through Virginia in the late summer of 1980, after many years spent outside the South, I noticed that we were passing tree after tree with large caterpillar tents hanging down from their branches. It was a slowed-down, drawn-out moment of recognition. That was how, when I was a child, my grandfather's modest grove of pecan trees had looked, infested and festooned with just such gauzy sacs. I could remember my grandfather standing on the porch of his house in Boston, Georgia, towering above me as he gestured out at sunset toward the ruined trees. Now I saw again *cocoons of caterpillars in pecans.*

Here was an interesting texture of sounds, crisscrossing but patternless. Words sometimes, through likeness of sound, become bound to one another by ties remotely like those of human kinship. This is not to propose that any *meaning* attaches to the sounds independent of the words. But the interlocking sounds do seem to reinforce and in some curious way to authenticate the meanings of the words, perhaps indirectly to deepen and enlarge them. A part of the very nature of poetry lies in this fact.

Nor was it an accident that this run of sounds had fallen out into an iambic pentameter. I have a temperament much tempted by difficulty and proscription, which probably harks back to childhood. No act had ever seemed quite so pure and challenging in those days as the one forbidden by authority. And lately, against the better judgment of practically everybody, I had been thinking of writing sonnets again, after a lapse of twenty years. The reputation of the sonnet for backwardness matched the reputation of the very region before me, which only recently had begun to come out from under its dark historic cloud. If public sentiment ruled against the sonnet and its pentameters, that was enough to draw me on. Already out of this one line many lines could be imagined flowing, many sonnets, an entire sequence, exploring and plumbing my sense of the South, whatever that might prove to be once I began work.

On the Porch

There used to be a way the sunlight caught
The cocoons of caterpillars in the pecans.
The boy's shadow would lengthen to a man's
Across the yard then, slowly. And if he thought
Some sleepy god had dreamed it all up—well,
There stood the grandfather, Lincoln-tall and solemn,
Tapping his pipe out on the white-flaked column,
Carefully, carefully, as though it were his job.
And they would watch the pipe-stars as they fell.
As for the quiet, the same train always broke it.
Then the great silver watch rose from its pocket
For them to check the hour, the dark fob
Dangling the watch between them like a moon.
It would be evening soon then, very soon.

But was this grandfather not less godlike than the actual one re-membered had in life been? And this effort to translate the mun-dane—pipe sparks and pocket watch—into the astronomical and cosmic seemed doomed to extravagance and sentimentality. Whatever sense of awe, whatever sense of encountering and being accepted into a world of mythic proportions might be pres-ent, was there, it seemed, only by force of will and desire.

There is always a drawer reserved for these disappoint-ments. With this one so painstakingly worked out, however, a clearer picture of what the other sonnets might be had be-gun to appear, not that in the event it would prove altogether accurate. In each, some half-archetypal or symbolic figure would be placed against a classic background or scene, this to be realized in exact and personal detail rescued from memory. The freaks and fantastics of recent Southern literature were to be shunned, the rhetoric of past glories choked off. If this meant sacrificing much by which the Southern in literature had come to be identified, the poems might claim to be no less true for all of that.

In my mind was a picture of my mother standing motion-less in bright sunlight beside the family plot in the cemetery in

Boston, Georgia. But was she weeping, or praying, or involved in something yet more hidden and mysterious? And did this picture come from memory or was it purely imaginary?

In any case, it has always struck me as a very pretty cemetery, a sort of fallen and faded Eden. The snake, last sighted in actual fact on a sunning-stone in some Carolina stream, hundreds of miles distant, was not to intrude upon this Eden until the last few lines. And the verbena *was* in bloom when last checked on, high and flourishing enough to harbor a busy invisible life. A mower at work downslope remained quietly and stubbornly in the text for weeks, rhyming with one thing after another. Otherwise the stillness was almost absolute, almost pure. The hummingbird showed its minute flash of red, and I wrote for line 8: "The ruby wing, or the stray clouds, or the cedar." But a student of mine, something of a naturalist, told me that no American hummingbird possessed such a wing color, and the family bird book confirmed my error. What had I really seen? Better to change the line. The very first version of this crucial line, incidentally, had been jotted down during a visit to the cemetery many months before, antedating even the "cocoons" line, but without any place then for it to fit: "Cedar and mockingbird and plastic rose." It has proved an extremely hard line to get right and to find a place for.

At some point I had copied out from Henry James's notebooks into a notebook of my own James's question concerning "the all abysmal," stopping with that phrase. (James was recalling a visit of his own to a cemetery in Cambridge, just across the river, coincidentally, from the Boston of the North.) It took the poet Henri Coulette to remind me of the sentences with which the James entry so movingly continues. Thus emerged the Medusa image.

Meanwhile I had begun to simplify the sonnet form, for convenience and novelty both. The usual crossing rhymes came down to a plainer stream of couplets, with the single exception of the rhyming pair connecting line 11 and line 14, a token nod to what might have been; and several of the rhymes were left—or made—purposely barbaric, as if to suggest the awkwardness of truth or some disdain for the artful. In line 2 the ellipsis was simply the print left behind by the vanished half-foot.

Some of the discomforts felt in childhood on my other grandfather's farm, just east of Tifton, Georgia, had come up in earlier poems. (In "First Death," for instance.) I could understand those feelings now as signs of alienation. One vivid memory was of sitting all afternoon in the sweltering front bedroom of that farmhouse at about age twelve or thirteen, alone, while everybody else seemed to be out working in the fields or off in the kitchen. I was reading a pocketbook anthology of poetry which happened to contain "The Ballad of Reading Gaol." I felt shut up in a sort of prison myself, filled with nameless small guilts and large longings. The attempt to memorize was bound to fail—I could never memorize—but it was the sign of some wish to establish my uniqueness, my difference. I felt isolated but superior, a prince in exile. The desecration of the hollyhocks must have been my secret revenge.

The normal pentameter of the sonnet is stretched out in "On the Farm" to a very long syllabic line having a strict count of fourteen. The first line itself, which had the sort of rhythmic run I wanted, became the model for this. Prose I was determined to avoid, and yet the very long line does pull toward prose. Most long lines having a fine speaking sound make use of pauses, often at a sort of balancing point near the middle of the line, but with a certain amount of interesting shifting about. (I had tried something like this before in a poem called "Mule Team and Poster.") A generous distribution of such pauses seems to be almost enough to keep the lines rhythmically alive and breathing. Along with the general pull toward prose, all rhymes soon dropped out, though by no means all interest in sound. These relaxed syllabics should stand out distinctly against the pentameters of the other poems, and vice versa.

As for "In the Train," the larger-than-life figure, not very specifically outlined, is a sort of Wolfean Telemachus, the adolescent romantic wanderer. But it is really the emotion, the welling up and crystallization of the ecstasy of travel, that grows to large proportion here. Since my own adolescence the images of Thomas Wolfe's night train journey had haunted me—a young man's author, if he is anything—and before finishing this poem I must have turned over, for the first time in decades, hundreds of his pages, making notes. Evidence of an aspiration toward sonnethood remains in the rhymes of lines 1 and 4. The writing was tuned up to as high a romantic pitch as anything I had done in years, somewhere up along the scale toward Wolfe himself, it may be. The climax, saved back as long as it could be, came with line 13—Wolfe's, with the tense altered—at which point the "sonnet" stops abruptly, one line short. But this sudden halt goes along with my conviction that poems ought to stop when they are done, and after the Wolfean apotheosis there was nothing more to be done or said. Using "we," I was joined again by my dead friend Robert Vaughn, the most profound romantic anyone can ever have wished to know, to whom at one stage the poem was tentatively dedicated. The two of us were, as it happens, on our way to nowhere more legendary than Manhattan. But Manhattan would do, for wonders and splendors; in fact, it did do.

The whole sequence aims to be transparent. The chief problem for a critic might be this very lack of difficulty, for I have observed that critics prefer to untie trickier knots. Yet history, biography, literature all do surround and underlie the sequence. In the absence of photographs from the family album, various picture books having the South as subject, such as Eudora Welty's, might fill in some of the background. Photographs from the Farm Security Administration of the thirties would be the right period, more or less, and have the right look. Many of them call back the sad beauty of the time and place.

Although they are obviously not sonnets such as could have been written in 1590 or 1820 or even 1950, the poems are no less obviously traditional. The lines *are* lines, with an integrity of their own, unlike most lines now being written. The meters have affected not just the composition and expressiveness of the poems but, for better or worse, can be seen as part of their very body and substance. For better, I would hope; inevitably and inextricably, in any case.

Political metaphors as applied to literary history can be objectionable as well as hackneyed, but they are convenient. In such terms the sequence can be called radically conservative, I believe, if we agree that this refers to an aesthetic position only and has absolutely nothing to do with politics. For one thing, meters now are taken to be the party badge of the conservative, and automatically so, by readers—often enough by poets themselves—who have very little understanding of how they work. The idea that art may possess an order and that life might be illuminated by that—even so basic and classical an idea as this—is considered unnatural, insincere, no longer up-to-date or relevant. But this looks like one of those moments when the most radical position of all—certainly the minority position, the position of the outsider—would be one that sought to carry on or to reconnect somehow with tradition. I think of the memorizers of forbidden books in the old Ray Bradbury fantasy, members of an underground. By tradition I do not of course mean Milton and Wordsworth only, but Hardy and Frost, Williams and Stevens, Baudelaire and Rimbaud, etc. The age of experiment is exhausted and moribund, temporarily at least. There is no one with the brilliance and authority of Williams, and the whole lineage that came after him seems to be wearing thin, like soil needing rotation. Meanwhile, much of American poetry is awash in a great ruck and welter of sentimentality. In most universities, most journals, the attitudes prevailing are attitudes left over from the sixties; but the sixties are dead. Let us consider instead the twenties and thirties: Brecht and Alberti, perhaps. Not Trakl or Rilke any longer now, however exalted or evocative, but rather the social realism and hard, definite outlines of Brecht. Not Neruda or Vallejo any longer now, however passionate and sincere, but rather the cooler technical brilliancies, the mysterious precisions of Alberti. A tradition could be put back together starting with not much more than this. Not forgetting rhythm; not forgetting truth.

GALWAY KINNELL
and
TED SOLOTAROFF

The Fundamental Project of Technology

"A flash! A white flash sparkled!"
—Tatsuichiro Akizuki,
Concentric Circles of Death

Under glass, glass dishes which changed
in color; pieces of transformed beer bottles;
a household iron; bundles of wire become solid
lumps of iron; a pair of pliers; a ring of skull-
bone fused to the inside of a helmet; a pair of eyeglasses
taken off the eyes of an eyewitness, without glass,
which vanished, when a white flash sparkled.

An old man, possibly a solider back then,
now reduced down to one who soon will die,
sucks at the cigaret dangling from his lip, peers
at the uniform, scorched, of some tiniest schoolboy,
sighs out bluish mists of his own ashes over
a pressed tin lunch box well crushed back then when
the word *future* first learned, in a white flash, to jerk tears.

On the bridge outside, in navy black, a group
of schoolchildren line up, hold it, grin at a flash-pop,
swoop in a flock across grass, see a stranger, cry,
hello! hello! hello! and soon, *goodbye! goodbye! goodbye!*
having pecked up the greetings that fell half unspoken
and the going-sayings that those who went the day
it happened a white flash sparkled did not get to say.

If all a city's faces were to shrink back all at once
from their skulls, would a new sound come into existence,

135

audible above moans eaves extract from wind that smoothes
the grass on graves; or raspings heart's-blood greases still;
or wails babies trill born already skillful at the grandpa's
        rattle;
or infra-screams bitter-knowledge's speechlessness
memorized, at that white flash, inside closed-forever mouths?

To de-animalize human mentality, to purge it of obsolete
evolutionary characteristics, in particular of death,
which foreknowledge terrorizes the contents of skulls with,
is the fundamental project of technology; however,
the mechanisms of *pseudologica fantastica* require,
if you would establish deathlessness you must first eliminate
those who die; a task attempted, when a white flash sparkled.

Unlike the trees of home, which continually evaporate
along the skyline, the trees here have been enticed down
toward world-eternity. No one knows which gods they
        enshrine.
Does it matter? Awareness of ignorance is as devout
as knowledge of knowledge. Or more so. Even though not
        knowing,
sometimes we weep, from surplus of gratitude, even though
        knowing,
twice already on earth sparkled a flash, a white flash.

The children go away. By nature they do. And by memory—
in scorched uniforms, holding tiny crushed lunch tins.
All the ecstacy-groans of each night call them back, satori
their ghostliness back into the ashes, in the momentary
        shrines,
the thankfulness of arms, from which they will go
again and again, until the day flashes and no one lives
to look back and say, a flash, a white flash sparkled.

Knowing and Not Knowing

I know nothing about how Galway Kinnell wrote this amazing poem, but I imagine that he came to it in the common way, drawing upon an image and a feeling that the nuclear age fosters in most of us. The image is that of the white light that I sometimes envision when I walk to work in the morning in Manhattan, the last thing I've been told I'll see before all these buildings and people and I disappear. The feeling is the one I have sometimes when I see one of my children in full relief and think of the precariousness of his future. These items of shared experience recur through the poem's patterns of observation, vision, and prophecy: the homing devices, as it were, by which Kinnell stays on his course through the dark imponderables of his subject.

The poem begins with a series of objects that one of the two atom bombs we exploded in Japan has turned into images and omens. By these we can begin to imagine and foresee. The poet begins pretty much where the reader is at, standing before some material objects, taking them in. The objects have certain things in common. (1) They are in a display case in a museum; they are relics: i.e., pieces of history as well as of matter. (2) They are human relics, most of them household items, or otherwise—like the eyeglasses or the skullbone inside the helmet—made for human use. (3) They are more or less global in nature; there is nothing particularly Japanese about these relics, nothing that trips the little protective device in our minds that distinguishes between them and us. (4) They are, with one exception, objects that are made by one or another heat process—cooking, forging, smelting—and hence have a high degree of heat resistance. This is also true of the exception, the relic of the once-animate object, the person whose skullbone was one of his most heat-resistant parts. Thus, if we are fully heeding the opening stanza, we must begin to imagine for ourselves a heat that transforms, melts, or otherwise alters glass, wire, helmet metal, human bone. (5) The items are unified in their meaning, semantically fused, as it were. The skullbone and the eyeglasses frame are of no more or less significance than the wires become iron lumps. In this glass case lies a small world of objects with only one common meaning which levels the distinctions between them— between glass, metal, and bone; between a thing and a person. Not even the relics of Pompeii are so tenaciously held in the grip of their event and so implacably signed by it.

The poet's voice in the first stanza is as neutral a medium as the glass through which one sees these objects, as impassive as the objects themselves. Just as they require our imagination to turn into deep images of an instant holocaust, so the tone is emotionally uninflected until we begin to read the lines with our own fear and pity. In these ways Kinnell counteracts the banality of another poem about the Bomb and also the underlying wariness, evasiveness, and dimness most of us bring to it. The objects speak for themselves; the poet appears at our side rather than on a platform. Part of the poem's power to move is in its sense of sharing rather than telling.

The structure of the first stanza, like that of the poem as a whole, is masterfully ordered and timed. It moves not only from the inanimate to the human images, that is from a lesser to a greater degree of identification (in both senses of the word), but also from a lesser to a greater degree of emotional implosion. For example, note the sequence of verbs, which grow more expressive as significances begin to hit home. This is accompanied by the slowly rising rhythm that thrusts aloft the final three verbs—"taken off," "vanished," and "sparkled"—leaving them to brood over the latent desolation and terror of what has come before and to anticipate what is to follow. That is to say, the wholeness of the poetry creates a rising movement from objectivity through pathos and into mystery. This is a traditional movement of prophecy, which the rest of the poem will follow.

II

The figures of the next two stanzas, the old man in the museum, the schoolchildren outside, carry the pathos forward, connected as they are by the scorched school uniform, the crushed lunch box. But the poem is also moving quietly toward prophecy, and these figures are placed in an unfolding visionary field that distinguishes between them. In his recent book *The Gift*, Lewis Hyde develops the distinction between the two Greek words for life—*bios* and *zöe*. The former "is limited life, characterized life, life that dies." The latter is "the life that endures; it is the thread that runs through bios-life and is not broken when the particular perishes." The old man is seen mainly under the aspect of bios-life: subject to its accidents, he was elsewhere when the white flash sparkled; subject to its fate, he will soon die. However, as a human being he bears the imprint of generic, possibly genetic, feeling: as naturally as he might gaze into a fire, he sighs over the memento of a schoolchild who died that day. The schoolchildren of stanza 3 are seen mainly under the aspect of zöe-life: they are as animated and collectivized as a flock of birds, they evoke the ongoing revitalization of life from generation to generation; vivid creatures of the here and now, they also fade into their counterparts in the preceding generation, those of the scorched school uniforms and crushed lunch boxes. With them and, to some extent, with the old man, Kinnell's sight is turned into vision, passes into the zöe-life and its eternal present—or rather what used to be before the word "future" first learned, in a white flash, to jerk tears.

The zöe-life is often invoked in Kinnell's poetry: the perdurable moment that resonates through time, the incandescent image that illuminates a universal: a boy sighting a pond for the first time from a high tree from which he is about to fall; four older men struggling to keep their doubles game going as night and winter settle over the court. By such images we can imagine the wider, mysterious context of our lives, can move outside the "small ego," as Hyde calls it, into the collective consciousness and experience, the solidarity we share as human beings. Such images also function decisively in the circuitry of the poem. The images of stanzas 2 and 3 work like a relay network, gathering up the meaning and feeling previously fused in stanza 1 and shunting it on ahead to the vision of unprecedented horror that unfolds. The relics are omens from the white flash, flashing from past to future as the poet's eye and imagination, seeing together, begin to foresee and envision, his consciousness to join the collective one of the race itself in its terrible new disjunctions. Or, more concretely, the life in the old man about to pass into the unknown and the schoolboy relics lead to the sudden appearance of the schoolchildren—creatures of renewal, but who are associated instead with the dead schoolchildren of Hiroshima. From this disjunction of the zöe-life in the poet's mind is engendered the prophetic question about an unprecedented sound on earth.

In the deep circuitry of the collective mind into which the poet has now tapped and through which the sense of the white flash obsessively flows, the brain-empacted helmet presages a whole city's population of faceless skulls; the earthly sounds of the old man's sigh, the children's goodbyes presage the sound of an ultimate final lamentation beyond any previous obsequies of the wind or of the human voice, even "the infra-screams" made at Hiroshima and Nagasaki. Thus stanza 4 mingles the bios- and zöe-life at the split moment of extinction of the human mentality. From this expanded and intensified network of images, layer upon layer, comes its prophetic meaning: the elimination of the creaturely terror of death by means of technology, the answer "*pseudologica fantastica*" offers to religion, humankind's previous way of coping with this foreknowledge and fear.

I noted earlier that one of the other conduits of the poem's manifold power is the movement of its tone from objecivity to pathos; in stanza 5, the irony that has delicately limned the tone—the old man smoking his way to death, the animation of the schoolchildren in *their* black uniforms, the "flash-pop" of the cameras—now moves front and center to present the berserk rationalism of the nuclear weaponry. Objectivity, pathos, and irony, playing effectively off each other, have particularly potent synergy: the eyes, the heart, and the wit working together under difficult circumstances, harnessing oppositions, modulating incongruities, making them resonate in the mind in a complete way. What is happening in the poet's consciousness he makes happen in ours, passes on the impact of his vision as well as its burden. The tone of the poem is again finely tuned from moment to moment; its development is cunningly timed to deliver the abstract proposition of stanza 5 as an appalling vision, on the one hand, and to dramatically contrast with and test the emotionality of what has gone before on the other. Or to put it another way, objectivity and pathos are fused and triggered by wit, producing that laconic/tragic note of which Shakespeare was the master and his Hamlet the ultimate spokesman, particularly when he is at the pitch of his vision. It is what Robert Penn Warren speaks of as putting the feeling of the work through the fire which proves it.

III

A third source of the poem's power lies in the development of its thought, the progressive widening of the consciousness in which its core image and feeling are held. Among the Herman Kahns and Albert Wohlstetters who think about the unthinkable, the trick is to narrow and reify the subject of nuclear war until writer and reader alike are sedated by statistics and terminology, not to mention ideology. Before we can blow up most of the earth and the human race, we must first shrink and numb our consciousness of them, beginning with that of death.

The tone of stanza 6 modulates out most of the previous irony to expand the context into a religious one, the widest one there is for contemplating the earth and mankind and our relation to them. Like the Japanese trees, the reader is "enticed down toward world-eternity" by the quiet contemplativeness in the language of this stanza, built by its sounds and slow cadences to produce a hush, as it were, in its mood. At the same time, the movement of consciousness is very rapid: the pseudologica fantastica of technology is whisked away and replaced by the ancient pantheism of the shinto and Zen's paradoxical ways of enlightenment, of knowing and not knowing, into which the poem's concerns are gathered.

Or so it seems to me. I know little about Japanese religion, but the poem instructs me well enough to grasp how Zen Buddhism too is a repository of the eternal present, invoked like a wise and ancient sage to minister to our disjunctions and apprehensions. Like the other world religions, Zen is a repository of the zöe-life from which we come and into which we return. Following the course of its cycle, the two generations of schoolchildren, the one killed, the other imperiled, merge as they go away by nature and by memory, ghostly surrogates of the children we hold gratefully in our arms and release helplessly to the future of the white flash and the end of both the bios- and the zöe-life.

It is very difficult to write about Hiroshima and about the ten thousand Hiroshimas that are poised to happen. The subject is at once banal, incommensurable, and heavily defended against. We truly know and do not know. But the pathos and terror of this poem make the awareness of our ignorance permanently more difficult to evade or dismiss.

ETHERIDGE KNIGHT

THE IDEA OF ANCESTRY

1

Taped to the wall of my cell are 47 pictures: 47 black
faces: my father, mother, grandmothers (1 dead), grand-
fathers (both dead), brothers, sisters, uncles, aunts,
cousins (1st & 2nd), nieces, and nephews. They stare
across the space at me sprawling on my bunk. I know
their dark eyes, they know mine. I know their style,
they know mine. I am all of them, they are all of me;
they are farmers, I am a thief, I am me, they are thee.

I have at one time or another been in love with my mother,
1 grandmother, 2 sisters, 2 aunts (1 went to the asylum),
and 5 cousins. I am now in love with a 7 yr old niece
(she sends me letters written in large block print, and
her picture is the only one that smiles at me).

I have the same name as 1 grandfather, 3 cousins, 3 nephews,
and 1 uncle. The uncle disappeared when he was 15, just took
off and caught a freight (they say). He's discussed each year
when the family has a reunion, he causes uneasiness in
the clan, he is an empty space. My father's mother, who is 93
and who keeps the Family Bible with everybody's birth dates
(and death dates) in it, always mentions him. There is no
place in her Bible for ''whereabouts unknown.''

2

Each Fall the graves of my grandfathers call me, the brown
hills and red gullies of mississippi send out their electric
messages, galvanizing my genes. Last yr/like a salmon quit-
       ting
the cold ocean—leaping and bucking up his birthstream/I
hitchhiked my way from L.A. with 16 caps in my pocket and a

monkey on my back. and I almost kicked it with the kinfolks.
I walked barefooted in my grandmother's backyard/I smelled
    the old
land and the woods/I sipped cornwhiskey from fruit jars with
    the men/
I flirted with the women/I had a ball till the caps ran out
and my habit came down. That night I looked at my grand-
    mother
and split/my guts were screaming for junk/but I was almost
contented/I had almost caught up with me.
(The next day in Memphis I cracked a croaker's crib for a fix.)

This yr there is a gray stone wall damming my stream, and
    when
the falling leaves stir my genes, I pace my cell or flop on my
    bunk
and stare at 47 black faces across the space. I am all of them,
they are all of me; I am me, they are thee, and I have no sons
to float in the space between.

The Belly Dance

Who's filled to the brim on the gantry
For the dance begins in the belly.
                                    —Francois Villon

I made/up/ the poem, "The Idea of Ancestry," in the early sixties when I was in prison, in "The Belly of the Beast." The initial creative/impulses for the poem occurred—and many of the lines were made/up—during one of my many stays in Solitary Confinement, which is generally known as "The Hole." During the eight years I spent in prison (out of a ten to twenty-five years sentence for armed robbery), the Hole became as familar to me as my cell. Prison. Bars. Steel. Silence. Violence. Being in prison is, in itself, a *trip*—especially in the sense of oppression, on all levels; and, being in the Hole, the prison within the prison, is smothering—almost like being smothered in a grave. The Breath/is/ taken away; it /is/ hard to breathe in in the Hole.

. . . I am being shoved into the Hole. I am stripped naked, even to my socks. The concrete floor is cold to my feet. Keys are klanking and four or five guards are standing around; and, as always—more than any/other/place in prison—the sharp odor of *lysol*. I am given a blanket, and the steel door behind me is shut and locked. It is dark and chilly in the Hole: the walls are grey/steel, the floor is damp; there/is/a shit-bucket in the corner, and nothing else.

The first/few/days that I'm in the Hole I am so filled with anger, fear, and hurt over whatever incident (gambling, marijuana, or the Politics of the Joint) that's caused me to be here, that I do not notice the smothering. I pace the dark space, do push-ups, masturbate, curse the guards and the gods. Five or six days pass . . . I begin to slow down, and the smothering starts . . . I sleep a lot—never long and deep—just nervous

147

catnaps. I twist and turn on my blanket on the concrete floor, and my mind is like a beehive: I hatch plots, concoct schemes; I dream and fantasize . . . But everytime my body touches the cold steel walls, or my feet slip onto the concrete, reality rushes in and the smothering gets worse . . .

After being in the Hole for a couple of weeks, not knowing night from day, I begin to loose track of time, the days, the weeks; I become disoriented, out of/touch/with myself, and almost out of breath from the smothering. So I start to re/ membering: my grandmothers, grade/school classmates, guys I'd been in the army with, and my Family, most of all. (I think Memory and Imagination are the Parents of Creativity. And, in my situation, with such a bleak future facing me, Imagination, if not altogether dead, was definitely crippled.) I was so disoriented, so desperate to regain a sense of my self, of who I was, and Memory was all I had to draw on. So I started to re/calling: family names, faces; I started to mak- ing/up/ lines and phrases out-loud, memorizing them, and I started to breathe again. Later, back in my cell, I finished the poem.

It seems to me that "The Idea of Ancestry" belongs to a body of poems that I have come to call *geneological*. (I didn't have the term in mind when I made/up/ the poem of course; like I've already said, if I had anything at all in *mind*, it was the desperate attempt, the urge, to grasp a sense of my/self, of who I *was*—right then.) By geneological poems I mean poems whose Authority? upon personal, and sometimes collective, history, as that history is revealed by the poet to the Reader or Listener. Now, sometimes, this revelation, this authority, might happen in a single poem, but usually it seems to a group of them. And I don't think an audience will very/much trust the poet until his or her genesis *is* revealed. In other words, the poet is obliged to let his or her audience know ex- actly where he or she is coming from. I know that I personally don't trust the social and political comments inherent in most poems until I know the poet's geneology.

There seems to/be/ two (probably more) characteristics that are highlighted in these geneological poems. The first is Intonation: at some point in the poem, or poems, the re/citing, the re/calling, of the Dead—and that accompanying authority—takes place. The past merges with the present, the Dead with the Living. When this occurs, a Leap is made, from the unique to the common, from the I to the We. The breath of the poet and the people come together via the poem, and this common breathing, from deep in the belly, causes a common motion, a common movement, a common Dance. Art is then happening. It's probably got a great deal to do with the mechanics and poetics involved in the sounds and rhythms of intoning, in the way the Words, themselves, are used—repetitiously, for instance.

The second character of these geneological poems I am calling Tradition, altho both characteristics are traditional. This aspect of the poem ties it to a specific time and place, thus further establishing historical Authority. For instance, in Yeat's "Blood and the Moon," he sings:

Blessed be this place and more blessed still this tower.
. . . .
I declare this tower is my symbol; I declare
This winding, gyring, spiring treadmills of a stair
   is my ancestral stair;
That Goldsmith and the Dean, Berkeley and Burke
   have travelled there.

That's what I mean. When the re/citing of names, and numbers, especially of the dead, merges with a time and place, a Communication begins: first, with those people who re/cognize an historical tie to the time and place and names cited. Second, with those people who re/cognize an historical tie to a time and place and people, other than those cited.

Again, all of this I've said above—I had /none/ of it in mind when I made up the poem. I made it up so I could breathe a little more, from my belly, when I was in prison.

MAXINE KUMIN

At a Private Showing in 1982

For Gillian Anderson

This loving attention to the details:
faces by Bosch and Bruegel,
the mélange of torture tools,
the carpentry of the stake,
the Catherine wheel,
the bars, spires, gibbets, pikes—
I confess my heart sank
when they brought out the second reel . . .

Anorectic Jeanne d'Arc,
how long it takes her
to burn to death in this picture!
When monks fast, it is called ascetic.
The film beamed on the dining-room wall
of an old brownstone
undergoing gentrification on Capitol Hill,
glass shards and daffodils
on alternate lawns,
harpsichord, bare board table,
cheese, nuts, jug wine,

and striding across the screen,
hauntingly young, unbowed,
not yet absurd, not yet insane,
Antonin Artaud in a bit part:
the "good" priest,
the one who declaims
"You are persecuting a saint!"
but does not offer
to die beside her.

And how is any of this
different today,
except now in color, and talky—
this prurient close
examination of pain,
fanaticism, terror?

Though the judges dress
like World War I British
soldiers in tin helmets
and Sam Browne belts,
though the music exactly
matches the mouthed words,
though Jeanne's
enormous wounded-doe's eyes
roll up or shut down
in hope, in anguish,
though Renée Falconetti,
who plays this part, was merely
a comic-stage actress
and never shows up on celluloid again,

though Artaud
tonsured for the set
walks the streets of Paris
in costume in 1928
and is mocked by urchins
and is peppered with catcalls,
what does it profit us?

Artaud will die in the madhouse
in terror for his immortal soul,
Falconetti will drop out of sight,
an émigrée in the Argentine,
we few will finish the wine
and skulk out on this spring night
together, unsafe on Capitol Hill.

A Way of Staying Sane

Most of my life-as-a-poet I have avoided writing poems about paintings, pieces of sculpture, sonatas, or other people's choreography out of a Calvinistic sort of purism, thinking always that to give in to the impulse to embellish another's art diminishes rather than enhances it. For how can the poet fail to encumber the object of the poem with adoration, or overlay it with private, not necessarily valid, responses? And then the poem runs the risk of growing claustral, precious, or turning into a mere intellectual exercise. Despite the exception that proves the rule—Auden's "Musée des Beaux Arts"—the temptation was one I sturdily resisted.

"At a Private Showing in 1982" breaks all my internal rules. It is based almost scene by scene on Carl Dreyer's early silent film "Jeanne d'Arc." The impulse to write the poem overtook me some days after I had had the actual visual experience. I found I could not get the cinematography, the actors' intensity, and the brooding musical score out of my head. So I set about exorcising the total event—not just the movie, but the setting, the social evening—by putting it on paper, a common enough practice. What I wanted to do initially at least was to come to terms with the movie's power over me, to go down into the maelstrom of my emotional responses to it—my physical repugnance to the fanaticism portrayed in it, and the sadism that fanaticism feeds—in order to discover what *else* the film was saying. Yet I had no sure notion I would find anything else. After all, I was entitled to my visceral response; wasn't it precisely what Dreyer had intended?

The poem began for me during a terribly barren time, which invested it with special authority. I was winding down from my year and a half as Consultant in Poetry to the Library of Congress, a somewhat embattled position in which I was sniped at several times by the right-wing princelings of dark-

155

ness. I had spoken out against increased military spending, accused the Reagan administration of lack of compassion for the poor, attacked institutional censorship (the Renwick Gallery had closed down its poetry readings after some flap over a supposedly "political" poem), and cited discrimination in high places, including the august library, where new appointments had brought the tally of men in the Council of Scholars to twenty-six, as against two women. For my offenses I had incurred the wrath of the Heritage Foundation, which cited me in their monthly newsletter as a pornographic poet. An essayist writing in *Harper's* magazine had mysteriously the same poem in mind. And, face to face, the librarian had accused me of abusing the hospitality of the library.

These digressive facts seem to me in retrospect to explain that my state of mind was rather more vulnerable than usual. I seized on the poem with a kind of fervor. It became something I "had" to write.

Something else was happening, too. More and more I was drawn to subjects that involve moral issues. I wanted to engage the necessary poems, not quite shunning the lyric form I love, but bearing down harder now, in middle age, on the "eternal questions," as Dostoevsky called them. I don't attribute this willingness to risk all to a surer sense of self, but simply to the inroads of time. The lyrics will come of themselves, three or four a year. But the difficult poems, the demanding position-paper poems, are unpredictable. Thus the extra sense of urgency when this one walked on the set.

I dedicated the poem to Gillian Anderson, a member of the music department at the Library of Congress, whose search of previously uncataloged material had turned up the original musical score for the film. A talented musician and conductor as well as archivist, Anderson devoted literally hundreds of hours to matching the music to the celluloid frames, rediscovering the synchrony composer and director had intended fifty-some years ago. Because I had been unable to attend the public showing, Anderson and her husband invited me to the private showing that the poem describes, under circumstances that were surely more claustrophobic than the original screening would have been. For here there was no escape. A guest in their house, I felt I had to sit through my discomfort. We had broken bread together, drunk wine. I was enormously sympathetic to Anderson's labor. I couldn't leap up and flee. No, better to stay and faint from the pain of it if need be.

I am groping my way saying all this. I don't really believe that a poem deserves this lengthy foreground of explication. (And of course I didn't faint.) I would want my readers to be concerned with the words on the page, not with the poet's apologia, a kind of foreplay. And yet—and yet—is it ego that demurs and yields, all in the same breath? Now that the notion of audience has crept in, best to deal with it. Interviewers always ask: what audience do you write for? The poet replies, with the solid arrogance of poets everywhere: first of all, I write for myself. I feel that I am sufficiently hard to please, that the first obligation of the poem must be to answer to its creator. Beyond this, virtually all poets will declare that they write for that "perfect audience of one"—the ideal Other Out There, who will be profoundly touched by the poem. I try not to think much about audiences. I worry that thinking about them is next door to writing directly *to* them, either down or up. Soon comes such a prickly awareness of the listener or reader that the poet begins to be swayed this way and that way, led into dancing the jig. From jigging to pimping for the poem is only a half-step, and fatal.

There is something else to be said about the poet's sense of audience.

Increasingly, the poems that we write are poems about the death of society, the collapse of the planet, the end of everything human we have been taught to believe in, to build from, to aspire toward. I use the plural pronoun because I think my moral dilemma as a poet is rapidly becoming every artist's dilemma. Thanks to modern technology, we can watch the world's local wars on television. We can see the torture and the killings in color, even as they happen. Salvador is an example, but it is only one of many mind-numbing grisly situations around the world. What use do we make of this pounding on the doors of our perception, this battering of rationality? Why do we persist with our poems of anger and lament, even as we know that poetry "makes nothing happen"?

I write these poems because I have to. I wrestle with my own notions of human depravity in this, and in other poems, not because I think the poem can change our foreign policy, soften the heart of the military-industrial complex that feeds on first-strike potential propaganda, or arouse the citizenry to acts of civil disobedience for peace, but because, for my own sanity (and yours, and yours), I must live the dream out to the end. It is important to act *as if* bearing witness matters. To write about the monstrous sense of alienation the poet feels in this culture of polarized hatreds is a way of staying sane. With the poem, I reach out to an audience equally at odds with official policy, and I celebrate our mutual humanness in an inhuman world.

In the poem under discussion, raw feeling was not enough. Had it not been for the presence of Artaud in the film, I wonder if I would have been able to complete the poem. He was the catalyst in an earlier poem of mine, called "In April, in Princeton," a very formal set piece written in matching stanzas of three couplets apiece on which I had imposed the added constraint of finding a way to insert the words "in Princeton" in each stanza. It had begun as a kind of ornament, an act of fealty for the semester I had spent so happily in that luscious, wealthy community. But Artaud, whose work I had been reading in my big, bare office, invaded and saved the poem. To encounter him young, strong, and sane in this old film was a tender reexperiencing of the bond I had felt some years earlier when I read the sad drama of his death in the madhouse.

Gillian Anderson and I talked about the picture, too. She provided me with slightly erroneous information about Renée Falconetti. In the original draft of the poem I had the actress dropping out of sight in Brazil. The *New Yorker*'s eagle-eyed research staff saved me from this pratfall, however.

A word about process. At first I simply jabbed at the typewriter keys to put down everything I knew about the movie, the actors, my own despair, and so on. This is the way I usually work. Ordinarily, I don't feel safe about starting a poem

until I have two or three single-spaced pages of lines, frag-
mented phrases, facts or imagined facts spread out on the
desk. Then, I like to think, I can go inside and begin to find
the poem. But this time the poem went through only four or
five drafts before it congealed for me. The line length estab-
lished itself early on, as did the loose ''paragraphing'' of the
stanzas. On the whole, much less attention to form than to
passion, except for my insistence on working in a short, even
a staccato, line. I'm not sure why. Was I so involved in the
film that I didn't want to impose any further patterns on it?
Did the abrupt lines move for me somehow the way the film
moved from frame to frame? Most of my struggle with revi-
sions centered on how to deal with the chronology of the
piece. Should the now-first stanza be the second stanza? (It
was, through three versions.) Should I bring in Artaud later,
much later in the poem? (Initially, he didn't arrive in the
poem until after Renée Falconetti is named.) At what point
should I confess I could hardly go on with the screening? I ob-
sessed over this point, then blurted it out in the opening
stanza. And the ending tumbled into place almost at once—a
rare event, but one that almost always guarantees that the
poem will be carried through.

The rhyming patterns in the poem are so haphazard as to
appear unintentional. I'm not sure I approve of this new lax-
ness, though I think it imparts an immediacy to narrative
that helps propel the reader through the poem. I find I am
doing this dangerously often now—detail / Breugel / tools /
wheel / reel /—and even: takes her / picture / ; offer / beside
her. This is breezy, freewheeling, associative slant rhyme.
Part of me feels it should be legislated against, but the other,
permissive part loves it for the easy flow. God knows where it
will lead me, down what primrose path the old formalist in-
side me will now stumble.

I find myself hoping that this is the first of some poems that
will take a new direction, engage in a dialogue with political
situations, with moral concepts and contemporary dilemmas.
There is no way to know that in advance. So I sit back like the
old hunter, waiting for the bear to pass this way.

STANLEY KUNITZ

The Abduction

Some things I do not profess
to understand, perhaps
not wanting to, including
whatever it was they did
with you or you with them
that timeless summer day
when you stumbled out of the wood,
distracted, with your white blouse torn
and a bloodstain on your skirt.
"Do you believe?" you asked.
Between us, through the years,
from bits, from broken clues,
we pieced enough together
to make the story real:
how you encountered on the path
a pack of sleek, grey hounds,
trailed by a dumbshow retinue
in leather shrouds; and how
you were led, through leafy ways,
into the presence of a royal stag,
flaming in his chestnut coat,
who kneeled on a swale of moss
before you; and how you were borne
aloft in triumph through the green,
stretched on his rack of budding horn,
till suddenly you found yourself alone
in a trampled clearing.

That was a long time ago,
almost another age, but even now,
when I hold you in my arms,
I wonder where you are.

163

Sometimes I wake to hear
the engines of the night thrumming
outside the east bay window
on the lawn spreading to the rose garden.
You lie beside me in elegant repose,
a hint of transport hovering on your lips,
indifferent to the harsh green flares
that swivel through the room,
searchlights controlled by unseen hands.
Out there is childhood country,
bleached faces peering in
with coals for eyes.
Our lives are spinning out
from world to world;
the shapes of things
are shifting in the wind.
What do we know
beyond the rapture and the dread?

The Layers

Only a few months ago a graduate student at a Midwestern university sent me an elaborate commentary on an early poem of mine, requesting my seal of approval for his interpretation. Since I could scarcely recall the lines in question—they had been produced in my twenties—I needed first of all to reacquaint myself with them, almost as if they had been written by a stranger. Something quite disturbing happened to me. As I began to read, the apparent subject matter crumbled away, and what I heard was a cry out of the past, evoking images of an unhappy time, the pang of a hopeless love affair, in a rush of memory that clouded the page. When I turned to my correspondent's thesis, I found that a large portion of it was devoted to an analysis and classification of prosodic devices, fortifying his perception of the poem as an example of metaphysical wit. Such discrepancies are not isolated occurrences. The readers of a poem perceive it as a verbal structure, about which they are free to speculate; whereas the poet himself is irrevocably bound to the existential source.

This is not to imply that the knowledge of a poem's occasions makes it fully explicable to its maker. The work of the imagination is neither wholly conscious nor wholly rational. In my later years I have wanted to write poems that are simple on the surface, even transparent in their diction, but without denying that much of the power of poetry has its origins in the secrecy of the life and in the evocativeness of language itself, which is anciently deep in mysteries.

One of the great resources of the poetic imagination is its capacity to mount thought on thought, event on event, image on image, time on time, a process that I term "layering." The life of the mind is largely a buried life. That is why the ideal imagination, i.e., the Shakespearean one, can be compared to Jerusalem or Rome, cities sacred and eternal, great capitals

165

built on their ruins, mounted on successive layers of civilization.

As for "The Abduction," which I have rashly promised to discuss, I must confess that I do not claim to understand it fully, and even if I did I should be disinclined to attempt an explanation. Instead I propose to offer an abbreviated report on what I am able to recognize of its origins in the multifoliate tissue of experience and memory. Since it is a recent poem, I have a distinct recollection of its gestation period, which lasted approximately seven months from the date of the first entry in my notebook to the final version.

To a poet of my age each new poem presents itself in a double aspect, as a separate entity demanding to be perfected and, conversely, as an extension of the lifework, to which it is joined by invisible psychic filaments. In this latter aspect, all the poems of a lifetime can be said to add up to a single poem.

Ostensibly "The Abduction" began for me in Provincetown in the middle of a summer night when I woke and turned to gaze on the face of my sleeping wife: "You lie beside me in elegant repose, / a hint of transport hovering on your lips." In the actual writing, these were my first lines. Some thirty years before, in another place and a different life, a similar circumstance had engendered the opening of "The Science of the Night":

> I touch you in the night, whose gift was you,
> My careless sprawler,
> And I touch you cold, unstirring, star-bemused,
> That have become the land of your self-strangeness.

It strikes me that in both "The Science of the Night" and "The Abduction," the epithet for the body abandoned to its night-self is "indifferent," a word less accusatory than poignant, born of the knowledge that when we are most ourselves, as in sleep, we are most withdrawn from others, even those we love. That capacity for withdrawal may be one of the conditions of the creative life.

I cannot remember exactly when I came across this relevant

passage in the letters of Henry James, but for a long time its eloquence has haunted my ears:

"The port from which I set out was, I think, that of the *essential loneliness of my life*—and it seems to me the port, in sooth, to which again finally my course directs itself. This loneliness (since I mention it!)—what is it still but the deepest thing about one? Deeper about me, at any rate, than anything else, deeper than my 'genius,' deeper than my 'discipline,' deeper than my pride, deeper above all than the deep counter-minings of art."

When I review the genesis of "The Abduction," its subterranean strategies ("counter-minings," in James's phrase), I see that there are two women in the poem, maybe three, combined into a single figure. The image of the woman stumbling out of the woods came to me in a dream, just as I have recorded it, two or three months after I had put aside, in discouragement, my initial lines. Physically she resembled the "careless sprawler" of "The Science of the Night," who had kept a guilty secret from me; but the scenario of her fantastic adventure clearly derived from a book I had been reading, written by a friend, about UFO abductions.* One of the documents in the book is the transcript of an hypnotic session with a subject named Virginia, detailing her encounter in a glade with "a beautiful deer . . . a mystical deer." I might add that among the books of my youth that fired my imagination were *Grimm's Fairy Tales*, Ovid's *Metamorphoses*, *Bulfinch's Mythology*, and *Sir Gawain and the Green Knight*. Shapeshifting remains for me a viable metaphor.

In the vaults of memory everything unforgotten is equally real. Echoes of what we have read, dreamed, or imagined coexist in the mind with remembrances of "actual" happenings. The experience of poetry itself is part of the reality that enters into the making of a poem. I venture that there is a connection, however tenuous, between my account of "the engines of the night thrumming" and Milton's mysterious evocation, in "Lycidas," of "that two-handed engine at the

---

*Budd Hopkins, *Missing Time* (New York: Richard Marek Publishers, 1981).

door,'' but I doubt that anyone else would even guess at the linkage. Somewhat more palpable, I suppose, is the rhythmic allusion, at the end of my poem, to Yeats's celebrated question, ''How can we know the dancer from the dance?''

''The Abduction'' came to me, in all its aspects, as a poem of transformation. Once the transforming spirit had asserted itself, a host of preternatural images, not all of which I can identify, arrived in a cluster. Certainly the view through the bay window and the apparition of the green flares belong to the distant summer of 1928, at Yaddo in Saratoga Springs, when the ghost of a child, the daughter of the house, who had drowned years before in the lily pond at the foot of the rose garden, invaded my chamber in the tower, shattering the casement—or so I believed. And just as certainly the vision of the bleached faces peering in at me goes even further back to the night terrors of my childhood in Worcester, where the wind-tossed branches of the elm scraped on the glass of the fatherless house.

Nothing that I have said is meant to suggest that a poem, any poem, is at best an inspired pastiche, reducible to the sum of its constituent elements. One has hoped against the odds that it is something more, something at once capricious, idiosyncratic, and whole; not only bits and pieces, not only parts of speech, not only artful play, but one's own signature, the occult and passionate grammar of a life.

DENISE LEVERTOV

Gathered at the River

For Beatrice Hawley
and John Jagel

As if the trees were not indifferent . . .

A breeze flutters the candles but the trees give off
a sense of listening, of hush.

The dust of August on their leaves.
But it grows dark. Their dark green
is something known about, not seen.

But summer twilight takes away
only color, not form. The tree-forms,
massive trunks and the great domed heads,
leaning in towards us, are visible,

a half-circle of attention.

They listen because the war
we speak of, the human war with ourselves,

the war against earth,
against nature,
is a war against them.

The words are spoken
of those who survived a while,
living shadowgraphs, eyes fixed forever
on witnessed horror,
who survived to give
testimony, that no-one

171

may plead ignorance.
Contra naturam. The trees,
the trees are not indifferent.

We intone together, *Never again,*

we stand in a circle,
singing, speaking, making vows,

remembering the dead
of Hiroshima,
of Nagasaki.

We are holding candles: we kneel to set them
afloat on the dark river
as they do
there in Hiroshima. We are invoking

saints and prophets,
heroes and heroines of justice and peace,
to be with us, to help us
stop the torment of our evil dreams . . .

                    *

Windthreatened flames bob on the current . . .

They don't get far from shore. But none capsizes
even in the swell of a boat's wake.

The waxy paper cups sheltering them
catch fire. But still the candles
sail their gold downstream.

And still the trees ponder our strange doings, as if
well aware that if we fail,
we fail also for them:
if our resolves and prayers are weak and fail

there will be nothing left of their slow and innocent wisdom,

no roots,
no bole nor branch,

no memory
of shade,
of leaf,

no pollen.

"Gathered at the River":
Background and form

This is the prose of it: Each year on August 6 (and sometimes on August 9 as well) some kind of memorial observance of the bombing of Hiroshima and Nagasaki is held in the Boston/Cambridge area, as in so many other locations. Some years this has consisted of a silent vigil held near Faneuil Hall and other monuments of the American Revolution. Participants stand in a circle facing outward to display signs explaining the theme of the vigil, or pace slowly round, sometimes accompanied by the drums and chanting of attendant Buddhist monks. People stay for varying periods—there may be a constant presence for three days and nights. In 1982 the poet Suzanne Belote (of the Catholic radical peace group Ailanthus) and some others created a variation on this event. Participants (with the usual age range—babes in arms to white-haired old men and women) came to the Cambridge Friends' Meeting House for a brief preparatory assembly, then filed out to receive a candle apiece—thick Jahrzeit candles nailed to pieces of wood and shielded by paper cups—and proceeded to walk in a hushed column along Memorial Drive, beside the Charles River. The sun was low; a long summer day was ending. When we got to the wide grassy area near the Lars Anderson Bridge, where our ceremony was to take place, it was twilight. Shielding flickering flames from the evening breeze, we formed a large circle, into the center of which stepped successive readers of portions from the descriptions recorded (as in the book *Unforgettable Fire*) by survivors of the atomic bombings. A period of silence followed. And then "saints and prophets, heroes and heroines of justice and peace" —including Gandhi, Martin Luther King, A. J. Muste, Emma Goldman, Archbishop Romero, Eugene

Debs, Pope John XXIII, Dorothy Day, Saint Francis of Assisi, Saint Thomas More, Prince Kropotkin, Ammon Hennacy, the Prophet Isaiah, and many others I can't remember—were invoked. A form of ritual—an ecumenical liturgy—had been devised for the occasion, and as each such name was uttered by some member of the circle, the rest responded with a phrase that said essentially, "Be with us, great spirits, in this time of great need." The persons conducting the continuum of the liturgy turned slowly as they read the survivors' testimony, or statements of dedication to the cause of peace, so that all could hear at least part of each passage: for we had no microphones, preferring to depend on the unaided human voice for an occasion which had a personal, intimate character for each participant rather than being a PR event. Some music was interspersed among the verbal antiphonies, and the human atmosphere was solemn, harmonious, truly dedicated: from within it I began to feel the strong presence of the trees which half encircled us. Cars passed along Memorial Drive—slowed as drivers craned to see what was happening—passed on. A few blinked their lights in a friendly way, guessing from the date, I suppose, why we were there.

While we earnestly committed—or recommitted—ourselves to do all in our power to prevent nuclear war from ever taking place, it was growing dark. In the soft summer darkness details stood out: hands cupping wicks, small children's gold-illumined faces gazing up in wonder at the crouch and leap of flames, adults' heads bent close to one another as they clustered in twos and threes to relight candles blown out. And now the first part of the ritual was over and it was time to set our candles afloat, as they are set on the river in Hiroshima each year, that river where many drowned in the vain attempt to escape the burning of their own flesh.

People scrambled and helped each other down the short slope of the riverbank to launch the little candle-boats. Oblivious, a motorboat or two sped upriver, and minutes after a big slow wave would reach the shore. The water was black; the candle-boats seemed so fragile, and so tenacious. And all the time the large plane trees (saved from a road-widening project years before, incidentally, by citizens who chained themselves to their trunks in protest), and the other trees and bushes near them, were intensely, watchfully present. I have been asked if I really believe trees can listen. I've always thought our scientific knowledge has made us very arrogant in our assumptions. Wiser and older individuals and cultures have believed other kinds of consciousness and feeling could and did exist alongside of ours; I see no reason to disagree. It is not that I don't know trees have no "gray matter." It is possible that there are other routes to sentience than those with which we consider ourselves familiar.

The form of the poem: The title came from the literal sense of our being gathered there on the shore of the Charles, and also with the cognizance of the Quaker sense of gathering—a *"gathered meeting"* being, to my understanding, one which has not merely acquired the full complement of those who are going to attend it but which has attained a certain level, or quality, of attunement. Then, too, I had a vague memory of the song or hymn from which James Wright took the title of one of his books, and which I presumed must refer to the river of Jordan—"one more river, one more river to cross," as another song says. And though the symbolism there is of heaven lying upon the far shore, yet there is also, in the implication of *lastness*, of a final ordeal, the clear sense of a catastrophic alternative to attaining that shore. (No doubt *Pilgrim's Progress* was in the back of my mind too.) The analogy is obviously not a very close one, since survival of life on earth is a more modest goal than eternal bliss. Yet, relative to the hell proposed by our twentieth-century compound of the ancient vices of greed and love of power with nuclear and other "advanced" technology, mere survival would be a kind of heaven—especially since survival is not a static condition but offers the opportunity, and therefore the hope, of positive change. (For if one hopes for the survival of life on earth, one must logically hope and *intend* also the reshaping of those forces and factors which, unchanged, will only continue to threaten annihilation by one means or another.)

The structure of the poem stems as directly as the title from my experience of the event. The first line stands alone because that perception of the trees as animate and not uninterested presences—witnesses—was the discrete first in a series of heightened perceptions, most of which came in clusters. The following two-line stanza expands the first, more tentative observation, and places the trees' air of attention in the context of a breeze (which does not seem to distract them) and of the fluttering candles, which are thus introduced right at the start. Looking more closely at the trees, I see their late-summer color, but then recognize I am no longer seeing it, for dusk is falling—literally, but also metaphorically. The next stanza notes the largeness (and implied gravity, in both senses) of the trees, which it is not too dark to see, then again in a single line reasserts with more assurance the focus of my own attention: the trees' attentiveness. Following that comes the recognition of why, and for what, they are listening. The Latin words introduced here (echoing Pound's use of them) express the idea that "sin" occurs when humans violate the well-being of their own species and other living things, denying the natural law, the interdependence of all. (That usury belongs in this category, as Pound reemphasized, is not irrelevant to the subject of this poem, recalling the economic underpinning of the arms race and of war itself.)

My underlying belief in a great design, a potential harmony which can be violated or be sustained, probably strikes some people as quaint; but I would be dishonest, as person and artist, if I disowned it. I don't at this stage of my life feel ready for a public discussion of my religious concepts: but I think it must be clear from my writings that I have never been an atheist, and that—given my background and the fact that all my life George Herbert, Henry Vaughan, Thomas Traherne, and Gerard Manley Hopkins have been on my "short list" of favorite poets—whatever degree of belief I might attain would have a Christian context. This in turn implies a concern with the osmosis of "faith and works" and a sense of the sacredness of the earthly creation. That sense, not exclusive to Christianity, and deeply experienced and expressed by, for instance, Native Americans, is linked for Christians to the mystery of the Incarnation. To violate ourselves and our world is to violate the Divine.

The trees' concern, proposed with a tentative ''as if'' at the beginning, and then as an impression they ''give off,'' is now asserted unequivocally. Once more comes a single line, ''We intone together, *Never again*,'' focused on the purpose of our gathering; and the words ''never again'' bring together the thought of the Nazi Holocaust with that of the crime committed by the U.S. against Japanese civilians, a crime advocates of the arms race prepare to commit again on a scale vaster than that of any massacre in all of history. This association might carry with it, I would hope, the sense that those who vow to work for prevention of war also are dedicated to political, economic, and racial justice, and understand something of the connections between long-standing oppression, major and ''minor'' massacres, and the giant shadow of global war and annihilation.

The narration continues, up to the launching of the candle-boats; pauses—a pause indicated by the asterisk—as we hold our breath to watch them go; and continues as they ''bob on the current'' and, though close to shore, begin to move downstream. Like ourselves, they are few and pitifully small. But at least they don't sink. Like all candles lit for the dead or in prayer, they combine remembrance with aspiration.

Finally the poem returns its regard to the trees, with the feeling that they know what we know—a knowledge those lines state and which it would be silly to paraphrase. The single lines again center on the primary realizations. Indeed, I see that a kind of précis of the entire poem could be extracted by reading the isolated lines alone:

As if the trees were not indifferent . . .

. . . .

a half-circle of attention.

. . . .

We intone together, *Never again*.

. . . .

Windthreatened flames bob on the current . . .

. . . .

there will be nothing left of their slow and innocent
        wisdom,

. . . .

no pollen,

except that one absolutely essential bone would be missing
from that skeleton: the "if" of "if we fail." The poem, like the
ceremony it narrates, and which gives it its slow, serious *pace*
and, I hope, tone, is about interconnection, about dread, and
about hope; that word, *if*, is its core.

CZESLAW MILOSZ

Elegy for N. N.

Tell me if it is too far for you.
You could have run over the small waves of the Baltic
and past the fields of Denmark, past a beech wood
could have turned towards the ocean, and there, very soon
Labrador, white at this season.
And if you, who dreamed about a lonely island,
were frightened of cities and of lights flashing along the high-
     way
you had a path straight through the wilderness
over blue-black, melting waters, with tracks of deer and cari-
     bou
as far as the Sierra and abandoned gold mines.
The Sacramento River could have led you
between hills overgrown with prickly oaks.
Then just a eucalyptus grove, and you had found me.

True, when the manzanita is in bloom
and the bay is clear on spring mornings
I think reluctantly of the house between the lakes
and of nets drawn in beneath the Lithuanian sky.
The bath cabin where you used to leave your dress
has changed forever into an abstract crystal.
Honey-like darkness is there, near the veranda
and comic young owls, and the scent of leather.

How could one live at that time, I really can't say.
Styles and dresses flicker, indistinct,
not self-sufficient, tending towards a finale.
Does it matter that we long for things as they are in them-
     selves?
The knowledge of fiery years has scorched the horses stand-
     ing at the forge,

the little columns in the market place,
the wooden stairs and the wig of Mama Fliegeltaub.

We learned so much, this you know well:
how, gradually, what could not be taken away
is taken. People, countrysides.
And the heart does not die when one thinks it should,
we smile, there is tea and bread on the table.
And only remorse that we did not love
the poor ashes in Sachsenhausen
with absolute love, beyond human power.

You got used to new, wet winters,
to a villa where the blood of the German owner
was washed from the wall, and he never returned.
I too accepted but what was possible, cities and countries.
One cannot step twice into the same lake
on rotting alder leaves,
breaking a narrow sunstreak.

Guilt, yours and mine? Not a great guilt.
Secrets, yours and mine? Not great secrets.
Not when they bind the jaw with a kerchief, put a little cross
        between the fingers,
and somewhere a dog barks, and the first star flares up.

No, it was not because it was too far
you failed to visit me that day or night.
From year to year it grows in us until it takes hold.
I understood it as you did: indifference.

*(translated by the author
and Lawrence Davis)*

A Memorial

"Elegy for N. N." was written in 1962 but for a long time it remained in manuscript, as I hesitated whether to publish it at all. The poem seemed to me shamelessly autobiographical and, in fact, it tells quite faithfully a personal story. This is good, for poetry should capture as much reality as possible, but the degree of necessary artistic transformation is a delicate point. Fortunately, the person of whom I speak has not been named; nevertheless the situation is as melodramatic as only life is: I live in Berkeley; I learn through a letter from Poland that a woman with whom I once had a loving relationship died recently. There are several details significant for those who read the poem in the original. The house by a lake is "beneath the Lithuanian sky," which is enough to evoke an exodus of populations at the end of World War II when Lithuania found itself within the borders of the Soviet Union. "The horses standing at the forge, / the little columns in the market place, / . . . the wig of Mama Fliegeltaub" mean that in the neighborhood there was a little town and that many Jews lived there before 1939. They were doomed once Hitler's army entered that area.

A reference to somebody dear to the heroine of the poem (a husband? a brother? a son?) who became "the poor ashes in Sachsenhausen" presupposes a knowledge of some historical facts: Oranienburg-Sachsenhausen was a big German concentration camp located near Berlin. As the Nazis placed the Poles on their list of "inferior races" close to the Jews, many were deported there, with a poor chance for survival. By saying "You got used to new, wet winters," I clearly state that my heroine moved after the war from her province to the territories situated to the west, formerly German, which were offered by Stalin to Poland as a compensation for the territories he had taken from Poland in the east.

Thus, the poem moves on the margin of big events in the history of the twentieth century. For an American reader, that is no more than the history of Central-Eastern Europe. For me it is simply the history of our planet—and not because I am a Polish poet but because quite early, already at the time of World War II, consequences of what occurred in that part of the world could be foreseen. But, of course, when writing the poem I did not try to speak of history or to convey any message. I was following a true biography, while now I notice that the poem calls for copious historical footnotes.

There are two houses in the poem, one by a lake, another, probably on the shore of the Baltic Sea (''wet winters''), is a villa whose German owner has been killed, obviously in 1945, when the Soviet army overran that area in its march on Berlin. I ask myself whether I should now provide more information on those houses. The poem does not tell anything about how I became acquainted with them, whether I visited or lived there, etc. Images connected with those places are so vivid in my mind, I have so much to say on the subject, that my memory at once starts to spin a narrative amounting to a novel. Yet, even though I have written two novels in my life, I have never been able to get rid of uneasiness about that literary genre. After all, a novelist exploits most intimate details from his or her life in order to prepare a concoction in which truth and invention are indistinguishable. A great master of such brazen operations was Dostoevsky. For instance, in *Crime and Punishment* he took his recently dead wife, Masha, for a model when depicting crazy Mrs. Marmeladova, and, even worse, in *The Idiot* he made comic General Ivolgin tell a tall tale about the burial of his own leg and the inscription he placed on its tomb: the inscription, as we know today, was identical with that on the tomb of Dostoevsky's mother. To be able to sacrifice everything, even what one considers as the most sacred, for the sake of an artistic composition seems to be a mark of a born novelist. But a poem does not aspire to a gossipy reconstruction of individual lives. Every poem is to a large extent circumstantial, and some familiarity on the part of a reader with circumstances behind the scene may help, provided that certain limits are preserved so that enough of a *chiaroscuro*, of a mysteriousness, remains.

Information on the house by a lake that is contained in the poem itself must, I feel, suffice. It does not satisfy my craving for reality, yet I am aware of obstacles on the road toward capturing it. Social, political, psychological elements tempt us and tend to dilute that sort of conciseness which distinguishes poetry from prose. My commentary on the new home of my heroine would be even more prosaic. In 1945 I myself visited the "western territories" of Poland and to my surprise became an owner of a house previously belonging to a German: to explain why it was easy then to acquire a property— especially if you were a writer, a member of the Writers' Union—would need a whole treatise; as well as why property was practically worthless.

The poem does not explain what sort of relationship existed between N. N. and me. Love affairs betwen men and women are of an infinite variety, but stylistic means of expression at our disposal prove their inadequacy especially in that domain. The language tends to reduce individual cases to a common denominator proper to a given epoch. Lyrics of the sixteenth century sing of love that is not like ours; madrigals of the eighteenth century are imbued with a sensibility at which we look from a remote perspective. Similarly, love motives in the poetry of our time will be alien to the sensibility of the future. We may even suspect that a complex interplay of the mind and the flesh, making for a human sexuality so different from that of animals, constantly undergoes transformations that go together with transformations of the *Zeitgeist*. Of course, every poet is guided by Eros, who according to Plato is an intermediary between gods and men. Yet, considering the intricacies of our century, it is difficult today to write love lyrics. I have written a number of strongly erotic poems but very few addressed to a given woman. And "Elegy for N. N." is, for better or worse, an example of a rather reticent approach. It happens, though, that now, returning to the poem after many years, I discover its value as a memorial. I have brought her to life in a way, and now again I feel her presence.

I discover also that this is a sad poem. Think how many

dead are in it: N. N. herself; Mama Fliegeltaub, who was the owner of the only inn in the town and who stands for its whole Jewish population—as far as I know the Germans did not even care to deport them but executed them on the spot; a person close to N. N., who died in Sachsenhausen; a German owner of the villa. And all that just because I gave account of facts. But the saddest is the ending, and I am not sure whether I approve of it. Rather not, which would mean that I have changed since the time the poem was written. Indifference and a feeling of distance from the world of the living has been ascribed to the shadows of the underworld, inhabitants of Hades. Upon my arrival in Berkeley in 1960 directly from Europe, I was for a long time visited by a thought that the distance separating me from the places of my childhood and youth had something eerie in it, that perhaps I found myself, if not in Hades, at least on some unearthly fields among lotus-eaters—in other words, that I had started to lead a sort of afterlife. This found its reflection in the poem's last stanza. Which is invalidated by the rest of the poem. For N. N. visited me after all. And by writing about her, I proved that I was not indifferent.

STANLEY PLUMLY

Posthumous Keats

The road is so rough Severn is walking,
and every once in a while, since the season is
beautiful and there are flowers on both sides,
as if this path had just been plowed,
he picks by the handful what he can

and still keep up. Keats is in the carriage
swallowing blood and the best of the bad food.
It is early November, like summer,
honey and wheat in the last of the
daylight, and above the mountains a clear

carnelian heartline. Rome is a week
away. And Severn has started to fill
the carriage with wildflowers—rust, magenta,
marigold, and the china white of cups.
Keats is floating, his whole face luminous.

The biographer sees no glory in this,
how the living, by increments, are dead,
how they celebrate their passing half in love.
Keats, like his young companion, is alone,
among color and a long memory.

In his head he is writing a letter
about failure and money and the ten-
thousand lines that could not save his brother.
But he might as well be back at Gravesend
with the smell of the sea and cold sea rain,

waiting out the weather and the tide—
he might as well be lying in a room,

in Rome, staring at a ceiling stylized
with roses or watching outside right now
a cardinal with two footmen shooting birds.

He can still remember the meadows near
St. Cross, the taste in the air of apples,
the tower and alms-square, and the River
Itchen, all within the walk of a mile.
In the poem it is Sunday, the middle

of September, the light a gold conglomerate
of detail—"in the same way that some pictures
look warm." He has closed his eyes.
And he is going to let the day close down.
He is thinking he must learn Italian.

By the time they reach the Campagna the wind
will be blowing, the kind that begins at sea.
Severn will have climbed back in, finally a
passenger, with one more handful to add
to what is already overwhelming.

A Commentary

The life in detail, the small moment, the texture of a thing—
that, it has seemed to me, is where the poetry is. Whatever we
extrapolate, however we transform the event, we hold to
those first values of experience in which we can connect what
will later seem inevitable. Keats is in a hired carriage, a
vettura, on his way from Naples to Rome. He has less than
four months to live. It is November 1820, warm, wildflowers
everywhere. Severn, his companion, thinking to make more
room for his sick friend and tired of the rough ride, decides to
walk. His painter's eye cannot help but be attracted to the
color in the day—mountains, the sea, the Italian sky, the
fencerows of the vineyards, and, almost at their feet, blue and
white and yellow flowers. After the long, claustrophobic, tu-
bercular, and stormy voyage on the *Maria Crowther*, two
months from Gravesend to the Bay of Naples; after a typhus
quarantine of more than two weeks in a lie within teasing dis-
tance of their destination; after the long-suffering realization
that Keats is deeply and irrevocably ill; after the sea-cold and
the damp and the smell of death, the autumn countryside
feels like spring. The land trip north, in slow motion, will take
yet another week. Keats and Severn are tourists, but broke.
They won't eat well, they won't ride well, but they will *see*—at
one point, improbably, a cardinal, with two footmen also
dressed in red, shooting songbirds. And they will see, daily,
as if wildflowers were the motif of the mortal world, spread
after spread of color, right up to the Campagna.

Severn can't keep his hands off the flowers. Nor does he
know what to do with them once he's picked them. So he
puts them, by the handful, in the small carriage with Keats,
like company. This goes on, off and on, for days. By the time
they reach the outskirts of Rome, Keats is witness to his own

funeral. We can imagine the lunar aspect of his great face flush among the display. Severn's later report is that he "literally filled the little carriage with flowers." During the week's journey he likely filled it more than once. All the biographers, from Lowell to Hewlett to Ward to Bate to Gittings, include this passage from Naples to Rome, and they all, basically, offer the same information—the road was rough, the weather and countryside were beautiful, Keats and his companion traveled slowly, were poor, and occasionally, as in the case of the cardinal with his retinue, they saw sights unimaginable in England. Aileen Ward, in *John Keats: The Making of a Poet*, gives the further detail that the cardinal used an owl tied to a stick with a mirror around its neck as a lure. She quotes Severn that the real sport was in not shooting the owl. None of the biographers, however, makes the connection between the wildflowers and the carriage. Severn, in his notes, perhaps understandably, ignores it too. I thought the connection overwhelming.

It's not my habit to look for poems. I'd been reading biographies of and letters by Keats for better than a year, not steadily or by study but as one reads good fiction. Shelley's *Adonais* and Leigh Hunt's version of the poet-too-sensitive-for-this-world aside, the real story of the life of John Keats is a moving and complicated testimony. He seems to me the most contemporary of the Romantics, as much for his willingness to share his vulnerability in the letters as for his ability to transcend his limitations in the poems. He wanted to write epics and tragedies and allegories of the heart; instead, at his best, he wrote some sonnets, a few odes, and a lot of mail. Most of his work is fragment. Nearly all of the poetry we love was written within a matter of months, often in one sitting. Like the rest of us, he had life on a daily basis to deal with. He was constantly torn between his need for society and his desire for solitude; and when he wasn't nursing a sick brother, he was trying to manage a neurosis about money. His writing time was piecemeal, ranging from the fifteen-minute sonnet to weeks of self-denying, sometimes painful island isolation. For all his sensual intelligence and his genius for transformation, the idea and the body of death were firsthand, personal and clinical realities. He had made his choice between surgery and poetry, in spite of the fact that early on he realized that, like so many in his family, he was doomed—not simply to die young, but to fail.

When I first came across that moment late in the biography, with Severn "literally filling the little carriage with flowers," Keats's whole life seemed to back up behind it. No matter how many times the text had been turned over, this moment felt new. It was alive. The event was there, given, embedded in the narrative, in the sequence of a long journey. All I had to do was connect two things, as in a metaphor, to read the moment with my own eyes, and to celebrate the moment, in time. Yet for me to make a poem of it I had obviously to do more than simply repeat it. I had, in a way, to use Keats's famous word, to become disinterested, to invest in the material without indulging myself, to maintain some negative capability. Though nothing about him is sentimental, sweet Keats has been the subject of too much weeping prose and, as we see in Shelley and others to follow, several weeping poems. I had to find a way of cooling the material without making it cold. The form I chose—what I would call a colloquial blank verse, with a line now and then breaking at a variable four beats—allowed me to stabilize not only the story but a stricter level of speech. I wanted the poem to talk, but I also wanted it to speak, to *acquire* its formality. The form both forced and offered certain economies of information and detail; it gave me the chance to balance my own feelings about Keats, the generous, grief-journey of his life, against the silence of saying nothing and letting the moment go, or worse, letting it spill out into little more than prose. I thought the poem should be in quatrains because I didn't want it to move too quickly. I wanted the story to be permitted a periodic and predictable rest, so that even as the structure of the thing moved toward climax and closure, the emotion, the "overwhelming" sense at the end, might stay open, as if the tension of the forward motion of the story opposed to the counter motion of the music were still in the air.

I wanted the moment enlarged and I wanted it extended.

Such larger dimensions of time would depend on my giving over to Keats, at a strategic break, the point of view of the poem, which is what I do at the beginning of the fifth stanza. I let a little of his memory of the frustrations of the voyage run parallel with the frustration he feels about his family and money and career, all those losses he's left behind. I even let him fantasize his room in Rome, which will turn out, inevitably, to be no fantasy. But the real memory will be of his walks, the year before, in and around Winchester: "Now the time is beautiful. I take a walk every day for an hour before dinner and this is generally my walk—I go out at the back gate across one street, into the Cathedral yard . . . then I pass under trees along a paved path, pass the beautiful front of the Cathedral, turn left under a stone door way. . . . Then I pass through one of the old city gates and then you are in one College-Street through which I pass and at the end thereof crossing some meadows and at last a country alley of gardens I arrive, that is, my worship arrives at the foundation of Saint Cross, which is a very interesting old place, both for its gothic tower and alms-square. . . . Then I pass across St Cross meadows till you come to the most beautifully clear river— now this is only a mile of my walk." Two evenings later, September 19, in a letter to his friend Reynolds, he will write, "How beautiful the season is now—How fine the air. A temperate sharpness about it. . . . I never lik'd stubble fields so much as now—Aye better than the chilly green of the spring. Somehow a stubble plain looks warm—in the same way that some pictures look warm—this struck me so much in my sunday's walk that I composed upon it."

What he composed, of course, is his most perfect, his most richly complete poem, "To Autumn." Looking back, just fourteen months, it reads like a paradigm of the weather, the season, the countryside he now finds himself in, a season of mist and mellow fruitfulness, drows'd with the fume of poppies, while barrèd clouds bloom the soft-dying day. It's the poem in which he most disappears into the text, in which his own sense of the fullness and the contradictions of his life are brought to bear at the moment of transformation. The correlative is total. There's a wilderness to the poem, a fecundity, the emblem of spring absorbed by, overwhelmed by the greater emblem of autumn, but still present, like a taste or a chill. It's a poem of reconciliation, the wonder of acceptance. It's beyond victory or loss and the perishability of conclusions. It's that rare poem, a poem of deep happiness, held between stasis and process, at the source of memory. There's no evidence, though, that he took it very seriously. His mind was on saving his long poem *Hyperion,* now old news, by concentrating on the *Fall.* He was not, as we know, an epic poet; he was a lyricist. In rewriting this proposal of a poem, he barely made it to introducing his hero before it was over. As poetry, this wonderful fragment—*The Fall of Hyperion*—is almost a modern poem. It *sounds* different from the past. As autobiography, it announced the end of a career that had only begun. By October, Keats was ready to give up poetry altogether "and get employment in some of our elegant Periodical Works—I will no longer live upon hopes." His debts of all kinds were piling up.

He still had more than a year to live. This is the year, if one were writing a novel or building a play, that one would pay attention to. Whatever his health before, whatever his prospects as a man and as a poet, from now on his life was posthumous. And he knew it. By a slow, nearly measured declension, he began to divest himself of friends and the few entrapments of the life around him. Regardless of the apparent subject of the conversation or the lengthy letter, and whether in friendship or passion, the true, the underlying issue was always good-bye. No one, certainly not the English doctors, understood the depth of his illness—the fevers, the sore throats, the vomiting, the blood spitting were taken more as conditions of bad climate than conditions of bad health. Italy, in the eighteenth and early nineteenth centuries, was viewed as golden, the place where one got well, spiritually or otherwise. Keats did not want to go to Italy. He knew what the journey meant, even if those closest to him didn't. Over the course of the summer, 1820, he was practically pushed in the direction of the sea. The Italian cure was everyone's advice. Yet on the day of embarkation Keats was, effectively, alone. Severn had been collared only a few days before to share the trip—didn't all young artists want to visit the living Renaissance? On September 17, a Sunday, the boat went with the tide to Gravesend in order to wait out the weather in the channel. It was now exactly a year since he had walked the meadows near Saint Cross.

MICHAEL RYAN

My Dream by Henry James

In my dream by Henry James there is a sentence:
"Stay and comfort your sea companion
for a while," spoken by an aging man
to a young one as they dawdle on the terrace
of a beachfront hotel. The young man doesn't know
how to feel—which is often the problem
in James, which may have been the problem
with James, living, as he said, *in* the work
("this is the only thing"), shaping his late
concerti of almost inaudible ephemerae
on the emotional scale. By 1980,
when this dream came to me, the line spoken
takes on sexual overtones, especially since
as the aging man says it he earnestly presses
the young man's forearm, and in James
no exchange between people is simple,
but the young man turns without answering
to gaze over the balustrade at the ocean,
over the pastel textures of beach umbrellas
and scalloped dresses whose hems brush the sand,
without guessing the aging man's loneliness
and desire for him. He sees only monotony
as he watches waves coming in, and this odd
old man who shared his parents' table on the ship
seems the merest disturbance of the air,
a mayfly at such distance he does not quite hear.
Why should I talk to anyone? glides over his mind
like a cloud above a pond
that mirrors what passes over and does not remember.
But I remember this cloud and this pond
from a mid-week picnic with my mother
when I was still too little for school

and we were alone together
darkened by shadows of pines
when with both hands she turned my face
toward the cloud captured in the water
and everything I felt in the world was love for her.

A Phantasmagoria

In 1899, Henry James met Hendrik Andersen, his first love; eventually they would vacation in Newport together. In 1900, at the age of fifty-seven James wrote to another young admirer: "The port from which I set out was, I think, that of the essential loneliness of my life—and it seems to me the port, in sooth, to which again my course finally directs itself. This loneliness (since I mention it!)—what is it still but the deepest thing about one? Deeper about me, at any rate, than anything else, deeper than my 'genius', deeper than my 'discipline', deeper than my pride, deeper above all than the deep counter-minings of art."

The combination of this passage and the detail from James's biography is so obviously the starting point of my poem that readers may find the fact interesting that, at least consciously, it wasn't. When I had my dream and drafted the poem, I neither had read this letter nor knew anything of James's unhappy love affair with Andersen. The dream and the poem were in fact the impetus to find out more about James's life, and I didn't discover this information until much later, when the poem was nearly finished. Of course the discovery flattened me. Even the dramatic setting of the dream is the terrace of a beachfront hotel, presumably in a port where the two characters recently landed; in his letter, James uses the word "port" figuratively whereas the poem translates it into a literal place, as a dream might do with a remark heard during the day. And the subject of my poem is surely "essential loneliness," solitude and isolation (two very different things) set against the backdrop of a young child with his mother, and maybe this last scene is dug out of the dream in one of those "deep counter-minings of art" that James mentions.

I've given up trying to explain the coincidences, though I suppose I could have read James's letter somewhere years before and forgotten it. If so, it traveled some underground route through my psyche and acquired the texture and shape it takes in the poem. And if this is what happened, the generation of this poem, strange as it would have been, would have been less strange than otherwise and would be more traceable than most poems, or at least most poems of mine. They all arrive differently, indifferent to their origins, almost never fully grown, with their insistently particular set of character flaws and problems. Whatever useful and interesting things can be said about poetry, this part of it—its generation—seems to be a permanent mystery.

Yet there are great, persistent subjects. In *The Classical Tradition in Poetry*, Gilbert Murray says for the Greeks these were ''Love, Strife, Death, and that which is beyond Death.'' Loneliness, the port from which James set out, probably touches all these both coming and going. It does in his work, and I hope it does in mine, because this is what gives the subject universality and dignity. Otherwise, it is mere self-pity.

A poet probably has to get over his natural fear of self-exposure early if he wants his work to be neither precious nor opaque. In our culture, just the fact of having feelings at all in certain circumstances can be condemning enough, much less feelings that may not be agreeable. Genteel academic critics have always confused the beautiful and the agreeable in the poetry of their time; no less do they do so today. Eliot's notion that ''the emotion of art is impersonal'' was, in this sense, a defensive one, but it was also a way to suggest that the emotion should be the poem's, not just the poet's. In fact, the emotion must eventually be the reader's, and the only way to do this is somehow to embody the emotion in the poem. How this happens is finally as mysterious and infinitely variable as the poem's generation, but it seems to have something to do with the poet's ability to regard the poem as a thing apart from him at the same time his personal commitment to it is most intense. In any case, in the poems by other poets I love, the emotion is so personal that it seems to penetrate the superficial and not-so-superficial differences between us, the differences of sex, heritage, experience, of wholly different nations and histories. How incredible it really is to be touched by a twenty-four-year-old surgeon's apprentice dead a hundred and sixty years, or by a reclusive New England spinster of the 1860s, or by blind Homer, the anonymous bards of ancient Greece whose life and language must have been so unlike those of the United States in 1985 that in light of the one the other seems a dream. Or by the meticulous, impeccably toileted, fin-de-siècle Henry James, whose background and temperament could not be more different from my own.

Anyway, for the sake of the "impersonal" and however it came about, I was happy to be given the donnée of my poem. Once in 1980, I did awake with the sentence "Stay and comfort your sea companion for a while," spoken by an aging man to a young one, from a dream which—what can I say?—was authored by Henry James. Looking back now, I can see how the whole poem issues from that beginning, though these lines sat on, in, under, and away from my desk for about a year or so before they yielded much more of the poem. I only know how to work one way, from the first syllable to the last; as I get older I seem to be able to allow some of the syllables to temporarily satisfy me less in the belief that they may have an important role in the whole shape and in the hope that they will be changed into something better later on. The beginning of "My Dream by Henry James" gave me the characters and got the story going but, more importantly, made a slant on their content in language I found compelling. This of course is the main thing: what the language says is only part of what it is, and probably not the best part. I liked the sound, rhythm, and syntax of these lines, the rhymes, half-rhymes, and assonances such as "a while, dawdle, hotel" and "companion, aging man, young one" and "sentence, terrace." In free verse, the grammatical unit of the sentence almost has to dominate the rhythmical unit of the line, because the line doesn't adopt the identifying characteristics of end-rhyme or uniform meter. But free verse may allow an equally great richness of formal interaction of the words, and may therefore allow a different but no less complete instrumentality of the language. The greatest pleasure for me in writing poetry occurs when the form language acquires in arrangement vies for my attention with the meaning of the words, when the two in conjunction seem to be shaping each other. This is a bodily pleasure. It's a wonderful feeling when the form of a poem, the words themselves, seems to be telling you what the poem wants to be.

In the fall of 1980, about nine months after I first drafted "My Dream by Henry James," the Edward Hopper exhibit opened at the Whitney Museum. I was living in Princeton, New Jersey, and kept taking the train into New York to see it, and couldn't have said why much more exactly than could an animal that's drawn to a particular place. I loved the paintings, but there was something more in them I was looking for. They seemed both abstract and representational, that if you switched something in your brain a millionth of a degree you could see the picture of a tunnel or of the couple on the front porch in summer as a pure shape. I remember when I finally saw the paintings both ways at once; the form and the thing represented seemed to merge while simultaneously remaining distinct, and the tension between them became almost palpable, a physical sensation. I stopped in front of the painting I was looking at—it was *Approaching a City*—and prayed that somehow I would be able to do this in my poetry.

I worked on "My Dream by Henry James" off and on for the next year. I wrote it again and again from the beginning but couldn't finish it—literally finish it. I couldn't find the right ending, though I tried an embarrassingly wide selection. Then I tried to frame it differently—at one stage, the speaker became a critic who fell asleep in his office (bad idea); in another version, the young man's death in the First World War was foreshadowed (very bad idea). Et cetera. As I often do when all else fails, I began criticizing the poem in the margins before putting it away. "Use the language to direct," one draft says in block print, and "This is a thorough set-up and what the poem now needs is that move, or turn, inside." I was stuck in the dramatic situation of the dream, at the line "a mayfly at such distance he does not quite hear." I knew the poem had to go beyond or beneath the dream somehow, and had to do so with a kind of turn, or volta, the way a sonnet turns between the octave and sestet. All I had was an abstract sense of the shape and movement.

Is this why the scene that finally seemed right to me involves an image of arrested movement, of arrested time? And turns inside, into the speaker's memory, to the remembrance itself, and, further, into his feelings? I don't have answers to these questions. The poem tries to move through layers of association in a speaking voice that's capable of ornate criticisms in Jamesian diction ("shaping his late / concerti of almost inaudible ephemerae") and even quotes James's notebooks (" 'this is the only thing' "). But at the end something essential seemed called for, beneath elaborations and estrangements. If the poem does issue from its first sentence, I hope the last sentence absorbs and transmutes all that preceded it, denying none of the "essential loneliness" but shaping it. The "like" of "like a cloud above a pond" is, I think, the fulcrum that finally allowed the push into the speaker's mind, then into his memory, and ultimately, I hope, into his heart.

"There is always a phantasmagoria" said Yeats, and the word implies a rapidity of movement that seems to me essential to poetry. And when the poet is "most himself," Yeats continues, "he is never the bundle of accidence and incoherence that sits down to breakfast." If "My Dream by Henry James" works, whatever it has to do with me is probably the least interesting thing about it. Every poem has to be credible, and for most readers now this means they have to believe someone is speaking to them. Maybe at an extreme moment I was inhabited by the ghost of Henry James. I would like to think so. The poem is surely critical of him—to live *in* the work instead of in the world, I firmly believe, will eventually eviscerate the work. But this notion has many subtle complications, and it was also part of my intention in writing the poem to pay homage to James's many, many beautiful sentences.

LOUIS SIMPSON

Quiet Desperation

At the post office he sees Joe McInnes.
Joe says, "We're having some people over.
It'll be informal. Come as you are."

She is in the middle
of preparing dinner. Tonight
she is trying an experiment:
Hal Burgonyaual—Fish-Potato Casserole.
She has cooked and drained the potatoes
and cut the fish in pieces.
Now she has to "mash potatoes,
add butter and hot milk," et cetera.

He relays Joe's invitation.
"No," she says, "not on your life.
Muriel McInnes is no friend of mine."

It appears that she told Muriel
that the Goldins live above their means,
and Muriel told Mary Goldin.

He listens carefully, to get things right.
The feud between the Andersons and the Kellys
began with Ruth Anderson calling Mike Kelly
a reckless driver. Finally
the Andersons had to sell their house and move.

Social life is no joke.
It can be the only life there is.

*

In the living room the battle of Iwo Jima
is in progress, watched by his son.
Men are dying on the beach,
pinned down by a machine gun.

The marine carrying the satchel charge
falls. Then Sergeant Stryker
picks up the charge and starts running.

Now you are with the enemy machine gun
firing out of the pillbox
as Stryker comes running,
bullets at his heels kicking up dust.
He makes it to the base of the pillbox,
lights the charge, raises up,
and heaves it through the opening.
The pillbox explodes . . .
the NCO's wave, "Move out!"

And he rises to his feet.
He's seen the movie. Stryker gets killed
just as they're raising the flag.

*

A feeling of pressure . . .
There is something that needs to be done
immediately.

But there is nothing,
only himself. His life is passing,
and afterwards there will be eternity,
silence, and infinite space.

He thinks, "Firewood!",
and goes to the basement,
takes the Swede-saw off the wall,
and goes outside, to the woodpile.

He carries an armful to the sawhorse
and saws the logs into smaller pieces.
In twenty minutes he has a pile of firewood
cut just the right length.
He carries the cut logs into the house
and arranges them in a neat pile
next to the fireplace.

Then looks around for something else to do,
to relieve the feeling of pressure.

The dog!
He will take the dog for a walk.

*

They make a futile procession . . .
he commanding her to "Heel!",
she dragging back or straining ahead.

The leaves are turning yellow.
Between the trunks of the trees
the cove is blue, with ripples.
The swans—this year there are seven—
are sailing line astern.

But when you come closer
the rocks above the shore are littered
with daggers of broken glass
where the boys sat on summer nights
and broke beer bottles afterwards.

And the beach is littered, with cans,
containers, heaps of garbage,
newspaper wadded against the sea-wall.
Someone has even dumped a mattress . . .
a definite success!
Some daring guy, some Stryker
in the pick-up speeding away.

He cannot bear the sun
going over and going down . . .
the trees and houses vanishing
in quiet every day.

The Terms of Life Itself:
Writing "Quiet Desperation"

The ideas that make a poem present themselves as images. Their significance may not immediately be apparent and indeed may never be. But poetry does not wait on meaning, and certain things insist on being noticed, at times with the power of hallucinations. When I wrote "Quiet Desperation" the scenery was already in place, the situations familiar: a woman looking at a recipe as she prepared dinner; television going in the living room; sawing some wood for the fireplace; walking down to the water. There were houses overlooking the road, a screen of trees, and everything seemed to drowse in a sea light.

But poetry is more than description, just as a living creature is more than the sum of its parts. Poetry is a drama in which objects are cut loose from their moorings and sent flying to make their own connections. The first step, therefore, was to get my controlling mind out of the poem and treat the subject impersonally. So I embodied my ideas in a narrative—there would be a character to do the observing, and one or two others. The method isn't infallible—a particularly obstreperous ego will struggle not to let go, but writing about people in a narrative turns the poem away from the self and compels it to face the world.

I sent the man in the poem to the post office, where he met a man named McInnes who invited him to his house. I brought my character home and gave him a wife. They had a conversation in which she rejected McInnes's invitation, and this gave me an opportunity to express my own feelings about the narrowness of small-town life. Not only in small towns . . . the problem of how to get along with people sociably is universal. I write about a small town because in order to write

215

with conviction I must have a place in mind, and this is a set-
ting I know—it is where I live.

I had the man go into the living room, and gave him a son
who was watching John Wayne on television capture the is-
land of Iwo Jima. I enjoyed putting in the details, especially
"bullets at his heels kicking up dust." This is what machine
gun bullets do in movies. I like putting into a poem things
people accept as true—it is the pleasure Flaubert got from
quoting "received ideas." If you want to write poetry about
people, you must put in what they think, not just your own
feelings and opinions. Novelists know this, but these days
few poets seem to—they have little interest in the thoughts
and feelings of others. This makes for poetry with no ob-
served life in it and, of course, no humor.

When I put in John Wayne on Iwo Jima I had no idea how
this would tie in, but you have to let things happen and trust
there will be a connection. The more the poem seems to be
writing itself, the more joy you take in it. And if you can bring
it off, if the connections are there, you have a real poem, one
that lives and breathes by itself.

This is writing by impulse, and I know no other way in
which good poetry can be written. But you must be able to
trust the poem and withstand frustration. For the impulse
may flag and the poem cease to move. When this happens the
writer may try to forge ahead by sheer will, to think of some-
thing, to invent . . . Many poems are written in this way, and
the results are not good. They may look like poems, but they
are only exercises—they don't make you feel that they had to
be written.

I had come to such a place—could not see where the poem
was going. But instead of trying to make up something, I put
what I was feeling into the poem—my frustration.

Wordsworth said that poetry takes its origin from emotion
recollected in tranquillity. Readers have concentrated on the
recollecting, but the phrase "takes its origin" is just as impor-
tant. The act of writing begins with memory but is different
from mere recollection—it is a reconstruction of experience
with something added, the plus being the emotion of the poet
as he writes. The emotion that creates a poem is not the emo-

tion you had when you were having the experience, but the emotion you are having now, as you write.

If you write out of impulse, as I have said, it may leave you suddenly. Then,

> As high as we have mounted in delight
> In our dejection do we sink as low . . .

And now I was dejected and the poem was sinking. And still there was a pressure to write. I felt a kind of desperation.

This was what I put into the poem—I made the character feel my own desperation. Putting this feeling into the poem made it more than a description and gave it such depth and meaning as it has. It brought the character to life and made him interesting—to myself and, it has seemed, to others.

Many have known the dread that can come upon you suddenly, a cloud blotting out the sun. You are aware that life is passing, "and afterwards there will be eternity, / silence, and infinite space." Your pulse is racing and you feel a need to act, to stave off some disaster.

I once remarked in a poem that I could never think of anything to make my characters do. I meant this as irony, but a critic took it to be an admission of failure. When you are writing out of feeling, you don't have to make anything happen—the writing is interesting and the characters are alive, like Hamlet, though they are standing still. On the other hand, if feeling is absent no amount of plotting helps. The writing and incidents will not move.

In "Quiet Desperation" form follows feeling. The third part begins with "A feeling of pressure . . ." The sentence fragment and short line suggest that the pressure is overwhelming. A longer line follows:

> There is something that needs to be done

The next line consists of one word, "immediately." This is urgent and peremptory. Then there is a step down, the poem continuing to the right of the page. The form sags as the feeling sags:

>   But there is nothing,
> only himself.

There follows the reflection about eternity with its echo of
Pascal. Then the thinker pulls himself together and acts, the
short brisk lines evoking decisive action:

>   He thinks, "Firewood!",
>   and goes to the basement . . .

Having given my own anxiety to the character, I knew what
he would do . . . saw firewood, walk the dog . . . things I
had done myself on such occasions. Anything to relieve the
pressure.

He is walking past the slopes and woods of the landscape
celebrated by William Sidney Mount a hundred years ago in
his paintings of Long Island. As he walks he looks at the trees
and grass and the cove glimpsed through the trees. Nature is
beautiful.

But when he gets down to the shore he finds that garbage
has been dumped on the natural scene. There are daggers of
broken glass on the rocks. At this point I discover the rele-
vance of the battle of Iwo Jima. In a time of war the young
men who smash bottles and strew garbage would be heroes.
They have no education to speak of—our public schools have
seen to that. They cannot sit still and think. But they are full of
energy, so they get drunk and smash bottles. Or perhaps try a
bit of burglary . . . anything to break the monotony of their
lives. If there were a war they would go to it.

Not only in the States . . . millions of people all over the
world are suffering from boredom and what Baudelaire called
"spleen," a feeling of frustration, a rage at conditions, at the
terms of life itself.

Deprived of the opportunity to lead a company of marines,
Sergeant Stryker dumps a mattress on the beach and speeds
away in his pickup. It is a small victory over the forces of law
and boredom. Sergeant Stryker needs a war to keep him
going. He cannot stand the monotony of peace and the feeling

that his life is being spent to no purpose. But this is what life is—it is banal, and the rewards are fleeting. If we wish to live we must learn to withstand the banality.

My own solution is to write a poem—others will have other solutions.

What there is to say about the form and style of the poem may be said in a few words. The stresses within the lines are so variable that I would not call them feet. I do observe, however, a preponderance of lines with three or four stresses. The lines vary in length, and I pause at the end of the line or run on as I would if I were speaking. This kind of verse isn't entirely free and it isn't written in meter. The term I think best describes it is *free form*.

Writing in 1844, Emerson said, "It is not metres, but a metre-making argument that makes a poem—a thought so passionate and alive that like the spirit of a plant or an animal it has an architecture of its own, and adorns nature with a new thing."

"Quiet Desperation" is not free verse—the lines have marked rhythms, and the poem has form, or "architecture," to use Emerson's word, the form not predetermined but rising from the matter in hand. The term *free form* describes this kind of writing more accurately than *free verse*.

The voice of poetry is not the voice in which you say good morning or talk to the man who fills your gas tank—still, there is a connection. I agree with Wordsworth that poetry should be a selection—with the word "selection" emphasized—of the language people actually use. I listen as I write for the sounds of speech.

There are readers who want the images in a poem to be far-fetched, things we have not seen or heard. Others want a style that draws attention to itself. And there are those who estimate the value of a poet in direct proportion to his unwillingness or failure to make sense. For such readers my writing can hold little interest—I write about feelings people share, in language that can be understood.

W. D. SNODGRASS

Old Apple Trees

Like battered old millhands, they stand in the orchard—
Like drunk legionnaires, heaving themselves up,
Lurching to attention. Not one of them wobbles
The same way as another. Uniforms won't fit them—
All those cramps, humps, bulges. Here, a limb's gone;
There, rain and corruption have eaten the whole core.
They've all grown too tall, too thick, or too something.
Like men bent too long over desks, engines, benches,
Or bent under mailsacks, under loss.
They've seen too much history and bad weather, grown
Around rocks, into high winds, diseases, grown
Too long to be wilful, too long to be changed.

Oh, I could replant, bulldoze the lot,
Get nursery stock, all the latest ornamentals,
Make the whole place look like a suburb,
Each limb sleek as a teeny bopper's—pink
To the very crotch—each trunk smoothed, ideal
As the fantasy life of an adman.
We might just own the Arboreal Muscle Beach:
Each tree disguised as its neighbor. Or each disguised
As if not its neighbor—each doing its own thing
Like executives' children.

                        At least I could prune,
At least I should trim the dead wood; fill holes
Where rain collects and decay starts. Well, I should;
I should. There's a red squirrel nest here someplace.
I live in the hope of hearing one saw-whet owl.
Then, too, they're right about Spring. Bees hum
Through these branches like lascivious intentions. The white
Petals drift down, sift across the ground; this air's so rich

No man should come here except on a working pass;
No man should leave here without going to confession.
All Fall, apples nearly crack the boughs;
They hang here red as candles in the
White oncoming snow.

Tonight we'll drive down to the bad part of town
To the New Hungarian Bar or the Klub Polski,
To the Old Hellas where we'll eat the new spring lamb;
Drink good *mavrodaphne*, say, at the Laikon Bar,
Send drinks to the dancers, those meatcutters and laborers
Who move in their native dances, the archaic forms.
Maybe we'll still find our old crone selling chestnuts,
Whose toothless gums can spit out fifteen languages,
Who turns, there, late at night, in the center of the floor,
Her ancient dry hips wheeling their slow, slow *tsamikos*;
We'll stomp under the tables, whistle, we'll all hiss
Till even the belly dancer leaves, disgraced.

We'll drive back, lushed and vacant, in the first dawn;
Out of the light gray mists may rise our flowering
Orchard, the rough trunks holding their formations
Like elders of Colonus, the old men of Thebes
Tossing their white hair, almost whispering,

> Soon, each one of us will be taken
> By dark powers under this ground
> That drove us here, that warped us.
> Not one of us got it his own way.
> Nothing like any one of us
> Will be seen again, forever.
> Each of us held some noble shape in mind.
> It seemed better that we kept alive.

Apple Trees and
Belly Dancers

One favorite indoor sport among American poets is to take a much revered poem and set it to some outrageous popular melody—one whose rhythm fits the text, but whose sound ruthlessly desecrates it. At a party, the burning question may be, "What's the tune for Wordsworth's 'She Dwelt Among the Untrodden Ways'? The answer: *Yankee Doodle!* Someone may go past singing Donne's "Valediction Forbidding Mourning" to *The Syncopated Clock*. Or you'll hear comparative versions of "Stopping by Woods on a Snowy Evening" sung to *O, Tannenbaum*, the *William Tell* Overture, or—the master stroke!—*Hernando's Hideaway*. We are like lovers who dare express ourselves only in a sort of mocking raillery lest we be totally obliterated by our adoration.

Something quite opposite, though, once happened to me: a vulgar Broadway show tune took a decisive part in a quite serious poem I was writing; may even have lain behind its inception. In his essay "The Music of Poetry," T. S. Eliot wrote:

> I know that a poem, or a passage of a poem, may tend to realize itself first as a particular rhythm before it reaches expression in words, and that this rhythm may bring to birth the idea and the image; and I do not believe that this is an experience peculiar to myself.

I can corroborate his claim—though I'm not sure he would welcome an example using belly dancers, transvestites and strippers, a bunch of wormy old apple trees, and a cheap show tune. Couldn't I have picked something from the *St. Matthew Passion?*

Some years ago, I was trying some rhythmical and metrical experiments, adopting musical forms to poetical uses. I had

225

noticed that Whitman often uses a sort of theme-and-variations device in building the rhythmic structure of a poem. Often, in his first line, he states a rhythm, repeating it with slight variation for the second half. The poem, then, is built upon this twice-stated rhythm, playing with it, lengthening, stress-loading, altering, sophisticating it. The resultant structure of rhythms *is* that poem's music, intimately involved with its structures of imagery and rhetoric.

The finest example, of course, comes from his book *Sea Drift:*

> Out of the cradle / ⏑ ⏑ / ⏑
> endlessly rocking, / ⏑ ⏑ / ⏑

Among American poems, only the *Song of Myself* is greater; none is more perfect in its beauty. So long and complex a piece, of course, uses many other devices as well, especially after the first verse paragraph where this rhythm so dominates as nearly to override the dictionary sense. For this poem, interestingly enough, the process took place in almost the opposite order to what Eliot suggests. The poem was first collected in the third (1860) edition of *Leaves of Grass,* where it begins:

> Out of the rock'd cradle, / ⏑ ⏑ / / ⏑

This line remains unchanged in 1867, although much is changed and tightened in the lines which immediately follow it. The rhythmic theme which we find so remarkable in the poem as we now know it first appeared in a handwritten, but rejected, version of the first line for 1867; the present first line did not appear until the fifth edition in 1871. That is, Whitman had worked out the variations of ll. 2–22 *before* arriving at the theme, the present first line. Even more remarkable, that rhythm's return in the poem's penultimate line, just when you've almost forgotten it—one of the most hair-raising moments in any poetry—only appeared in the seventh edition of 1881.

My first venture along these lines was a long poem about

Van Gogh's *The Starry Night*. Instead of a rhythm, it used the pattern of vowels and consonants of the painter's last recorded words, "Zóó heen kan gaan," which are also the last words of the poem.

Encouraged by my work on this poem, I decided to try working with a rhythm, though I wanted one markedly different from any of Whitman's. Shortly before this time, I had raised an orphaned baby Great Horned Owl. For this poem, "Owls," I took the call of the adult owl as my basic rhythm:

> HOO, hoo HOO, HOO, HOO

and went on to build variations on that:

> Wait; the Great Horned Owls . . .

My real concern here, though, is with the poem that followed, "Old Apple Trees." For some time before this, I had been trying to write about the overgrown orchard on our property. I had tried several different meters as well as a long-lined free verse, but nothing worked. Now I picked a theme—at random, I thought—to use for a set of variations:

> ⌣ / ⌣ ⌣ / /

Almost at once I found the poem coming with surprising speed.

Perhaps if I go back and scan the first eight lines, their rhythmic derivation—and that of the rest of the poem—will be obvious.

Like battered old millhands	⌣ / ⌣ ⌣ / /
they stand in the orchard—	⌣ / ⌣ ⌣ / ⌣
Like drunk legionnaires,	⌣ / ⌣ ⌣ /
heaving themselves up,	/ ⌣ ⌣ / /
Lurching to attention.	/ ⌣ ⌣ ⌣ / ⌣
Not one of them wobbles	⌣ / ⌣ ⌣ / ⌣
The same way as another.	⌣ / / ⌣ ⌣ / ⌣
Uniforms won't fit them—	/ ⌣ ⌣ ⌣ / ⌣

Though later variants get far more drastic, the first three stan-
zas run easily enough—comparing my trees to men who've
been bent and misshapen through difficult lives. No doubt I
was thinking of such men as my upstate New York neighbors,
the ordinary farmers, postmasters, grocery clerks that I would
see in the Fourth of July parades. Somehow they would cram
their outsized stomachs, their bent backs and uneven legs
into their old uniforms; down the street they wobbled,
straggling, some in time with the band ahead, some with the
band behind, some serious as church, some grinning broadly,
all laced with liquid high spirits.

    As I look at my poem now, I suppose that I am really con-
trasting my orchard with that of a rich lawyer down the road
from me. His trees look like orchards *ought* to look: each about
twelve or fifteen feet tall, all lined up front to back, side to
side, diagonal to diagonal. By the time I've reached the phrase
"each disguised / As if not its neighbor," though, it's clear
even to me that I'm not talking about trees at all. I suspect I
am talking about some of my less admirable students. I am
certainly talking about the American middle class and its
failure to turn freedom and prosperity into creative
individuality—a failure disguised alternately by gaudy self-
displays of costume and manner, then by blameful demands
for still more freedom, more unfair advantages. Freedom
from outside pressures only leaves us to the scant mercies of
our inner drives. If I appear to be preaching, it is to a congre-
gation of one—myself.

    No doubt my poem is defending my battered old trees from
the reproach I feel in my neighbor's tidy and productive or-
chard. His trees have had all the advantages—so they look
just like each other. Each having the same basic drive toward
form, they come, when sheltered from the pressure of events,
to look almost mass-produced. My trees?—they look like no
trees you ever saw before. They were planted before the days
of fertilizer spikes and insecticide sprays; they reflect the dif-
ferences in soils, the differences in seasons. You couldn't
grow such trees today—once something's invented it can be-
come, actually, a necessity; now, any tree planted in that area

must be sprayed every two weeks or it will be dead in three. So my trees, however misshapen, have a certain heroic cast to me. One that I *did* cut down (it had lost a main branch; soon the rot would hollow it out) had a butt log twenty feet long and twenty-three inches in diameter! The sawyer had never seen anything like it; *you* never saw anything like the two-inch apple boards it gave me.

True, my trees don't give me apples—they give me red squirrels, quail, saw-whet owls. What could my lawyer's orchard shelter except one of those life-sentence chickens that never see dirt, never eat bugs, and fill our supermarkets with identical boxes of perfectly tasteless, perfectly sterile eggs? I grew up in this middle-class culture; I must at least admire some less sheltered, less regulated, more troublesome, perhaps dangerous fertility and growth. Something created from that (often deadly) struggle between the internal drive, the ideal form, and the unpredictable events and pressures of the world—that, I think, is the essential argument of my first three stanzas.

Something very strange happens, however, at the beginning of the fourth stanza—the poem changes its locale: "Tonight we'll drive down to the bad part of town." No doubt there are places in America where one could drive easily from the earlier rural scene into an urban setting like that which follows. But no belly-dance joint lies in driving distance of Erieville, New York. Actually, the poem's clubs and bars—their names slightly changed—were the places my wife and I had frequented when we had lived in Detroit, almost ten years before. Like all the intellectuals there, we were very fond of the Greek, Arabic, and Armenian belly-dance joints and spent much time there. They, too, were a respite from American middle-class life. Many of the people we saw there were recent immigrants; many were working-class people like those of upstate New York in the earlier stanzas—the "millhands" of line 1 may have been a pointer toward this. Still, it seemed odd to haul that scene into my apparently pastoral poem. Even as I did it, one side of my mind was panicking: "It won't work! That's ten years ago! Three hundred miles! The landscapes won't blend!" But, somehow, another part wanted that belly-dance scene and kept saying, ''I dare you!''

It was with a great sense of relief that I found, when I got to stanza 5, I could tie the two scenes together by returning to the farm and seeing our old trees there as like another kind of Greek dance—something that would be done in a Greek tragedy. I might comment, aside, that I have always suspected that the singing and dancing for Greek tragedies should be far livelier and wilder than those solemn chants and stately movements most readers assume. Besides, in mentioning the old men of Thebes, I wanted specifically to recall Euripides' *Bacchae* with its comic and terrifying vision of the old men girding their dry loins and white hair in ritual garments, then fettling their stiff old limbs out to try the Dionysiac rites and orgies. Thus, it might not be too far a leap from my belly dancers, from the Greek solo and line dances, from our old crone with her *tsamikos*, to the ancient Attic dance ritual.

This, in turn, allowed me to give my Chorus of Trees a little eight-line choral song to end my poem. Here, for the first time, I dropped that rhythm already established (as Whitman did at the end of ''Cavalry Crossing a Ford''). If this passage at the end *has* a metrical system, I haven't discovered it. As I look at it now, it seems to me that the very last line's rhythm,

$$\smile / / \smile \smile \smile / \smile /$$

with its early spondee, then a long loop of unaccented syllables followed by a near-spondee, may echo the frequent spondaic endings of the poem's earlier half-lines. I hope it does, but I had no such *conscious* intention at the time; I merely noted that it satisfied my ear and so questioned it no further.

I *did* discover something funny, though, about the rhythm of the rest of the poem. One day a student at a small college asked about this poem's rhythm. My answer startled me: ''It goes: da DA da da DA DA; da DA da da DA DA. You know, like that old show tune, 'Heat Wave': 'We're having a heat wave; a tropical heat wave.' '' Later, I wondered what ever brought so silly a song to my head—I could just as well have said ''Blues in the Night'': ''My mamma done tol' me, when I was in knee pants." Or, since I spend most of my spare time studying classical music, couldn't I have found some example *there*? Why *not* the *St. Matthew Passion*?

I had never even heard "Heat Wave" often except in a little night place in Saratoga, New York, called Jack's—a place that had a drag floor show and catered to black transvestites. Exactly as our Detroit intellectuals haunted the belly-dance joints, so the artists and writers from Yaddo haunted Jack's. In the floor show, there was a gorgeous black stripper who used that song for her theme: she was called merely "Heat Wave." All of us, sex-starved from the monastic existence of Yaddo under its dowager queen, tried frantically to start something, anything, with her. In vain—the only one of us she'd even talk to seemed the least sparkling, dumpiest-looking guy in the place. She would sit at a table with him for hours, discussing the best brand of single-edged blades, while the rest of us gnawed our knuckles in frustration!

No doubt I associated Jack's place and that black dancer with the belly-dance joints in Detroit—one of the very best dancers there (Princess Sahara: half Scottish and half Russian) had married one of my students; the best of all (Princess Baudía: half North African and half Kentuckian) was another black girl, another stunning beauty. And it must have been that rhythm, once it was well established in the poem, that brought such places, such dances and dancers to my mind and to my poem. It would be nice, now, if I could show a similarity between the rhythms of the two kinds of dance music. Too bad; I am familiar with most common belly-dance drum patterns and none bears any close relation to that of "Heat Wave."

It seems to me now, though, that that rhythm may have contributed very much more. I cannot prove this, but I am convinced that it must have been related, all along, to a whole sense of barbarous ritual that I feel in such places—and, in part, to a feeling that, like the old men of Thebes, I was having, after a dull and proper youth, a somewhat riotous old age. I remember once telling my analyst about taking another poet, a lay brother, to one of those joints and of being amused that, although *he'd* wanted to go in the first place, he'd become so uncomfortable that he'd had to leave. My analyst had asked, "But going to such places—isn't that really *your* religion?" I still don't think I have a religion, but put in those terms, I couldn't deny it.

As for a tune like "Heat Wave," it is, after all, about another sort of dance and dancer, and the most pronounced spondee of all comes down, if I remember correctly, on the name of that dance:

> She started a heat wave, by making her seat wave.
> The temperature's rising; it isn't surprising:
> > She certainly can
> > Can-can.

The can-can started, of course, in the low dives and brothels of Montmartre. And for all the song's commercial prettification and corruption, isn't it also hinting, in some way, at the orgiastic and barbarous, which we still see as a celebration of something which, if not holy, will nonetheless assuredly destroy us should we refuse its worship?

I used to own a record called *Bach for Percussion* on which Saul Goodman, then principal tympanist of the New York Philharmonic, had taken a quotation from the great musicologist Willi Apel—a quotation which I can now give only in rough paraphrase:

> A successful fugue is distinguished as much by the mutual independence and interdependence of the rhythms of its voices as it is by that of their melodies and harmonies.

Goodman goes on to argue that one might, then, remove a fugue's melody and still have a fugue; with a group of other percussionists, he proceeds to do just that. In several Bach fugues, each voice is taken by one percussionist; the result is enormously exciting and powerful. I used to play their Little Fugue in G Minor for friends, sight unseen, and ask them to guess what it was. Invariably, the answer was something like, Central African tribal music? East Asian? I recall my colleague, Baxter Hathaway, remarking about it that he couldn't help wondering if all really great art wasn't perhaps built upon some such deep construct of barbarous celebration, covered only by a thin veneer of melody—of civilization and reasoning. If that were so, wouldn't that be only one more way that art imitates life?

WILLIAM STAFFORD

For a Daughter Gone Away

1

When they shook the box, and poured out its chances,
you were appointed to be happy. Even in a prison
they would give you the good cell, one with warm pipes
through it. And one big dream arched over everything:
it was a play after that, and your voice found its range.
What happened reached back all the time, and the "octo,"
the "isped," and other patterns with songs in them
came to you. Once on the Yukon you found a rock
shaped like a face, and better than keeping it, you placed
it carefully looking away, so that in the morning when
it woke up you were gone.

2

You saw the neighborhood, its trees growing and houses
being, and streets lying there to be run on;
you saved up afternoons, voluptuous warm old fenders
of Cadillacs in the sun, and then the turn of your thought
northward—blends of gold on scenes by Peace River. . . .

3

It was always a show, life was—dress, manners—
and always time to walk slowly: here are the rich
who view with alarm and wonder about the world
that used to be tame (they wear good clothes, be courteous);
there are the poets and critics holding their notebooks

ready for ridicule or for the note expressing
amusement (they're not for real, they perform; if you
take offence they can say, "I was just making
some art"); and here are the perceivers of injustice; they
never have to change expression; here are the officials,
the police, the military, all trying to dissemble
their sense of the power of their uniforms. (And here
at the end is a mirror—to complete the show for ourselves.)

4

Now, running alone in winter before dawn has come
I have heard from the trees a trilling sound, an owl I
suppose, a soft, hesitant voice, a woodwind, a breathy
note. Then it is quiet again, all the way out
in that space that goes on to the end of the world. And I think
of beings more lonely than we are, clinging to branches or
        drifting
wherever the air moves them through the dark and cold.
I make a sound back, those times, always trying for only
my place, one moving voice touching whatever is present
or might be, even what I cannot see when it comes.

Breathing on a Poem

Something you are writing, after it is done, or begins to feel close to done, you can lean over and breathe on it and try to bring its main moves, its trajectory, into the center of your attention.

"For a Daughter Gone Away" invites me to attain some such perspective. Not that it strikes me as all that neat and orderly—to me, it is a troubling, rambling poem, not a model of unity by any means. But it gives me occasion to brood about considerations that relate to any poem. If I breathe on it now, I can get back to something of the feeling of shaping any work, or so I hope.

The care—the caring—in this poem strikes me: the person addressed is lucky, and evidence is given for that. Slowly, by means of local, private references, the lucky person emerges—playful, quaint, the kind of person who dwells on what has happened, who carries along through the years many quick allusions to family adventures—"what happened reached back all the time."

My feeling is that all the early part of the poem can survive its weaknesses, even its ineptness, even its random or odd words and events, just so its direction stays steady. It is almost as if the recaller of events can be willfully obscure and relaxed: nothing can go wrong, because there is forgiveness in the person addressed and faith in the person talking. Much more important to me, in this part of the poem, is an orientation of acceptance, and that quality may even be enhanced by "blunders" or ramblings.

Because the poem does ramble, reaches onward through sections, I helped myself feel orderly by numbering the parts. In the second part the scene extends to the neighborhood; and again all is easy—it even ends with "Peace River." The reaching for places and events in this poem came about natu-

239

rally: our family made many trips together, and one notable trip to Alaska, where the spaces and loneliness became part of our growing, and the names like Yukon and Peace River impressed us, became part of our common references. The keynote I feel in the early parts of the poem is security, sharing. The color is gold. The time is voluptuous.

But in part 3 certain firmer, sterner notes begin to enter. Not forcefully, but with confidence, allusions to other parts of society crowd into consciousness: other artists are coolly recognized, officials are considered and neither attacked nor admired, "perceivers of injustice" exist—they just exist—not admired, not ignored. Elliptical though this section is, I feel it as that part of the growing-up process that carefully moves toward judgment. Not until considering the poem at this remove do I feel the slightness of this portion, the audacity of its presuming to have a part in the poem, with its slim, weak, almost imperceptible touches of irony, its caution, but its refusal to skip over a needed development in such a poem as this is beginning to be.

At the end of the section one sentence attempts to ward off a whole element of risk in growing up and becoming wise: there is a mirror so that we can see ourselves under the same kind of light we have been using for other people.

By now as I breathe on this poem I feel apologetic, and for a strange, completely unanticipated reason—it is far too ambitious. Whatever justification it might have as a responsible piece of discourse depends on most tenuous hints and connections. Can it be that poetry often allows both writer and reader to swing wide on allusion and hint and loose connection, just because only by such recklessness can one reach far out for meanings, with frail helps from language? At any rate, here in the fourth section I find myself introducing my feelings and thoughts, at last, in first person. And my role in this section is to signal the pulling away of a parent, the accepting of departure, the manifesting of a continuing easy experience, taking what comes, speculating on it. . . .

I think the last part is lonely, but is not reaching out to reclaim, and is "always trying for only / my place."

Phrases like that last, they surface in poems. They are

sometimes oddly inconspicuous, but it may be that the furniture of a poem, the emphasized parts, the prevalent elements, are not at all the main *motor:* a poem may provide you occasions for saying things that are so much a part of your life that you import them into even the most remote utterances. I now believe that in this poem I was blundering along through sections that offered me occasions for a few intense impulses of my own—ideas like these: you can be lucky even in prison, you can treat experience as a set of surprises on which to exercise your quirky self, you can welcome kinds of life that others might feel cheated by.

And now here at the last of my breathing on this poem I realize that in a high-handed way I used the writing of it to arrive at a statement that is spookily central to my kind of writing and to the aim of my life—the attainment of ''one moving voice touching whatever is present / or might be, even what I cannot see when it comes.''

GERALD STERN

Baja

These tiny Mexican mosquitoes are like lost souls
looking for blood among the white visitors
in their own land. They come to lead us through
some four or five old trees. They stoop to bite
our hands, they make that wailing sound I live
in terror of, they sing in our ears, they walk
between the seams, they reach for the drink they love,
they bend half over drinking,
they walk along the sand and through the flowers,
they look for work, they are looking for work, they pound
on the windows of our casita shouting *trabajo,*
trabajo, casting mournful eyes on the sea-wrack,
touching the broken sewer line and pointing
at the broken steps.
                          I catch one in a bottle
of Hellmann's and I let it loose outside
on the little plaza where the Citation is parked.
I tell him, my blood is for you, I tell him, remember
one Pennsylvanian who stopped to talk with the souls
and listened to them even if there was murder
and hatred between us; I ask about my future
as if I were Odysseus in hell
and he were Tiresias, that dear old lady,
or some other dead one, a Hercules or an Ajax.
He tells me, I think, to look out for my own
soul in the years to come, he tells me how long
it will be before I can rest a little, although
what he calls rest it may be some other thing
he talks about. He tells me there is a tree
and a yellow rock and a cloud. I should go left
around the tree, I should walk over the rock,
I should walk under the cloud; it is a Mexican

vision, full of darkness and secrecy.
I thank him for his kindness. Maybe he said
there is a room with terrible noises, tie
yourself to the kitchen table, hold your left hand
over your mouth, concentrate on living
a week at a time, divide your life into threes,
the terror can be digested, take care of yourself
when you are in New York, when you are sleeping,
when you are dying, there is a life to come—
or maybe he said, I love you more than anything,
have pity on me, please help me, take me with you,
I want the chance to live again, I can't
believe how large your limes were, oh I can't
believe how huge and clean your markets were;
take me with you, take me with you, wailing
and howling in front of me, in back of me,
pulling me down, the way they do, a swarm
of spirits, stumbling, pushing; I had to run,
I had to slam the door, I stood there freezing,
blood on the walls where I killed them, blood on my palms,
my forehead foolishly pounding, my two hands shaking,
all alone in the darkness, a man of the heart
making plans to the end, a screen for the terror,
a dish for the blood, a little love for strangers,
a little kindness for insects, a little pity for the dead.

A Seer

Like many other writers of this century, my obsession has been with the lost and neglected forces of the world, what is dark and hidden, and unseen, although I'm not sure if my own passion is the result of political or psychological or religious impulses, or a particular combination of the three. I find myself drawn to weeds and waste places and to ruined and despised cultures, especially when they are on the periphery of our great cultivated centers. The abandoned has been the subject, and to some degree the obsession, of all romantics, but it's not just the celebration of the lost and ineffable I'm interested in, but the terrible and irreconcilable juncture, if I can put it that way, of the two great poles, and the aesthetic and ethical and metaphysical consequences for all of us, even as I write of the sad and frightening consequences for myself alone. I have written many times about burned and destroyed places. I have been drawn to them. Sometimes I think it is merely the Gothic in me, but when I am in the presence of these places my tone and posture, I notice, isn't wonder or amazement or fear. It is sadness, but is sadness born out of a kind of familiarity. I am at home there, in the invisible place, every bit as much as I am at home in the visible. It is altogether domestic to me.

The most familiar analogue for this is the Freudian metaphor of the two states, particularly Freud's own version of *I* and *It*. Although the cry for Dionysius, coming as it did as a reaction against bourgeois self-deceit and shallowness and distorted and ridiculous Apollonianism, is perhaps just as common and useful, just as familiar. A thousand writers, from the profound to the silly, bombard us with notions of a war between the head and the heart, the rich and the poor, the male and the female, the present and the past, work and play, north and south, sun and moon. The longing for an authentic life, the battle against the father, the struggle with technology and imperialism and fatuous and shallow philosophies, are a part of the war, as is the return to nature, the search for the spirit, and the cultivation of ninety fresh forms of love.

I spent seven years on a long crazy poem called "The Pineys," where I explored the relationship between the Piney and the president, the Pine Barrens and the White House, those two modes of existence. The Pineys were the inhabitants, or imaginary inhabitants, of the Pine Barrens of southern New Jersey—illiterates living in squalor—as an old-timey social worker named Elizabeth Kite called them. She invented the term in 1912. I thought, at the time, that the Pineys could "carry" all the thoughts and feelings I had then about the "other," the neglected and repressed, just as I thought the White House could carry my feelings and thoughts for the dominant controlling forces. I ran into a few technical problems and shelved the poem, but I am still moved by the two presences in conjunction with each other. I have written and thought about weeds endlessly, and I have written and thought about burned-out buildings. I found myself at one point writing about a wrecked early nineteenth-century house in New Brunswick, New Jersey, while wandering through the old agora in Athens. It was the close ruin that appealed to me, not the far ruin. It was the empty bottle of Night Train Express and the carton of Salems and the 1950 plush car seat, not a tile from Phaistos or a marble foot or a three-thousand-year-old curlicue. It was the juncture and the closeness. Seen ironically and hopelessly in the light of the permanent. And whenever I'm on the way to the Jersey shore, to Atlantic City, say, or Long Beach Island, and I begin suddenly to see the stands of pitch pine and the dark cedars, I am overcome with an intense feeling, as if I were in the presence of the holy—I can't say less—combined with a certain joy and knowledge and peace. At the same time I have the insider's secret delight in knowing all about those trees and the long and lovely history of the region and where the rivers begin and end and where the roads are and the dark old bars and the ancient factories. Haunts of the unconscious.

I think I'm always on the brink of this subject, but from time to time I find myself confronting it directly. I think, in "Baja," I did that. I wrote the poem in March 1983, while spending a week with a friend in a little Anglo resort town halfway down to Ensenada. It was called El Mision. The parents of one of my students—they are from San Diego—own one of the houses in town and gave us the "casita," rent free, for our stay. It was, of course, attached to the main house and was only a few dozen feet from the ocean, down some steep steps. There had been tremendous, almost unheard-of storms all during February and early March, which not only made our visit problematic but which, when we did get there, cast a kind of mystic pall over the whole area because of the wreckage and the shifting of the shoreline. It was not an ordinary visit to a rich and colorful Mexican village on a wonderful cliff overlooking a blue sea. Seaweed, wood, dirt, glass were everywhere. Pipes were broken, walls were smashed. The water was cold and dirty and thirty, forty feet farther in than it ordinarily was. The beach was ruined, and what sunshine there was had a sinister rather than a healing or beneficent aspect to it. It was as if it were unseemly for the sun to be shining amidst that quiet horror, the sun that we closed our eyes in, and bathed in, and smiled up at. Clouds and gray skies were more appropriate. And a strong wind.

I don't know if the poem itself began with the persistent little Mexican mosquitoes or with the beautiful brown-eyed boys knocking on our window early in the morning looking for work. John, our host, referred to the mosquitoes as "mavericks," as if their burden or destiny were someplace else and they had somehow strayed from the mainstream and landed on our walls, and on our cheeks and hands. They weren't *supposed* to be there, what with the screens and the spray, those little malcontents, those radicals. Of course, neither was the sea supposed to break loose and the windows in the house on our left to be smashed, and the furniture in the house on our right to be delivered up to the waves. As for the Mexican boys, they were truly just looking for work, and whatever suffering they or their families had experienced from the storm, there was a kind of windfall for them in the way of unexpected income, since their help was desperately needed. Not only that, but the severe storm isolated and clarified the radical difference between them and the gringo visitors and their respective abilities to *"ride* the storm," just as it pointed out the tenuous and delicate hold of gringo culture on that little strip of rock and, by inference, mankind's hold in general on all the strips of rock and his control over nature and his civilized domain over chaos. What we call Chaos.

The central episode of the poem and the vehicle for carrying the theme is Odysseus's visit to the dark place and his negotiating with Tiresias for information concerning his return to Ithaca. Tiresias seems to me to be silly and pompous, the way fortune-tellers and entrail-stirrers usually are. He foretells the future just as Homer made him do, leaning on his golden staff, this trafficker in blood. Only what he foretells has a somewhat meaningless, somewhat frantically petulant and pedantic air about it, for he is not only Tiresias, he who sees both ways, the wisest of humans, he is also a mosquito, buzzing words of terror and mystery in our ears. In Tiresias's case the blood came from a black lamb, "handsomest of all our flock"; in the mosquito's case it came from a mournful and trusting poet, but it was blood in both cases that made them rest a little from their eternal wandering and gave them the power to speak and prophesy. But my mosquito is not just one of the ghostly dead; he is also a Mexican boy begging for work and he is a maverick and he is a weed and he is a source of deep annoyance. Under other circumstances he could even be waving a little machine gun and wearing fatigues. I assume the identity with Odysseus with a certain reservation for he is not my all-time favorite character in literature, though I do have admiration for him. He is conservative, and a protector of the laws, and a spokesman, indeed the chief spokesman, for tradition and for order—for civilization itself—in spite of his slightly wild, almost disorderly mien. The old Greeks could tolerate a little more frenzy than we repressed Viennese. Perhaps no scene in literature so reveals the two poles and their proximity and their hopeless and final disjuncture as Odysseus's visit to hell. And perhaps no other statement is clearer than Homer's: the two worlds, though they may be temporarily joined by the sharing of the life-force of the one, have separate destinies, though they are connected—and interconnected—in a terrifying and tragic way. The mosquito—as spokesman—longs for the blood, and the possessions, of the strange other world. For a moment we forget how noxious and irritating and repugnant his world is, and we are reminded how it leans on ours and longs for it—imagine!—this very world that so bores and angers us. And for a moment we are almost allowed to entertain the thought that it could be one, as Wendell Willkie and John Lennon sang, and we could—once again?—live in concordance and not worry about evil shadows, and even share our limes with each other.

As far as the politics goes, it exists on quite a literal level. The dark and despised force is Mexican—poor Mexican—living, at least there, by the mercy and largesse of the rich Americans. The presence of the Mexicans is very brief—they are doing their morning rounds looking for work—but they are ever-present, they are subsumed in the "person" of the mosquito, especially in the mosquito's most human and pitiful aspect, where he begs me, the visitor to his land, to take him with me, to the place in the north where the limes are large and the markets are huge and clean and he will have the chance to live again, without arrogant border guards this time, and a hideous Tijuana. To fuse the Mexican and the mosquito this way, not to mention Tiresias, is a little dangerous. If I go too much one way I am inhuman and exploitative; if I go too much the other way I am sentimental; and either way I am a little ridiculous. What I had to do was let the figure itself "carry me." Yet if he were a mosquito, smash him on the wall, and if he were a Mexican, then not die from agony and guilt. What saved me, frankly, was my belief in my own metaphor. I was carried away. I was temporarily insane. I shall never forget how thoughtful and generous that maverick was, in his bottle of Hellmann's. If he took blood from me, it was because he had to—that is how he sang. And if I protected myself, I was only doing what Circe had prepared and warned me to do in order to return from that place intact. "Take care of yourself"; "hold your left hand / over your mouth"; "I love you more than anything." All this he said to me in a voice I shall never forget. For a drop of blood, which cost me almost nothing. Which I have back, with his love; and his devotion; and his wisdom; that sweetheart, that poor lovely seer.

LUCIEN STRYK

Awakening

Homage to Hakuin, Zen Master, 1685–1768

I

Shoichi brushed the black
on thick.
His circle held a poem
like buds
above a flowering bowl.

Since the moment of my
pointing,
this bowl, an "earth device,"
holds
nothing but the dawn.

II

A freeze last night, the window's
laced ice flowers, a meadow drifting
from the glacier's side. I think of Hakuin:

"Freezing in an icefield, stretched
thousands of miles in all directions,
I was alone, transparent, and could not move."

Legs cramped, mind pointing
like a torch, I cannot see beyond
the frost, out nor in. And do not move.

III

I balance the round stone
    in my palm,
turn it full circle,

slowly, in the late sun,
    spring to now.
Severe compression,

like a troubled head,
    stings my hand.
It falls. A small dust rises.

IV

Beyond the sycamore
dark air moves
westward—

smoke, cloud, something
wanting a name.
Across the window,

my gathered breath,
I trace
a simple word.

V

My daughter gathers shells
where thirty years before
I'd turned them over, marveling.

I take them from her,
make, at her command,
the universe. Hands clasped,

marking the limits of
a world, we watch till sundown
planets whirling in the sand.

VI

Softness everywhere,
snow a smear,
air a gray sack.

Time. Place. Thing.
Felt between
skin and bone, flesh.

VII

I write in the dark again,
rather by dusk-light,
and what I love about

this hour is the way the trees
are taken, one by one,
into the great wash of darkness.

At this hour I am always happy,
ready to be taken myself,
fully aware.

What? Why This. This Only.

Up in my eyrie-room atop the Chapel of the Madonna of Monserrato, perched on a cliff higher than the hawks above Lake Como, listening to the sweet bells of Bellagio's San Giacomo, I begin to cast into air and mind for an explication of "Awakening," a poem written years ago in homage to the great Japanese Rinzai Zen master Hakuin.* He expressed more fully than any before or since, through art, painting as well as poetry, the transforming power of Zen discipline. The poem attempts through the relationship of seven parts to suggest the nature of the Zen quest. I shall try to give an idea of each part, without apology but with sharp awareness that most such attempts are foredoomed. When the sequence came, however, I felt I was giving body, shape, to impulses born of my meeting with Zen.

I

The artist Shoichi is brushing an *enso* (mystic circle, Zen's mandala), symbolizing Zen attainment. Often a poem is brushed above the *enso*, which in Japanese up/down script resembles "buds" rising from a bowl (image of the circle). In the second stanza, "pointing" suggests a mind sharply directed, the bowl—referred to as an "earth device"—the earth itself. Buddhist meditators often focus upon stone, water, stick, etc. The last part of the poem refers to an awakening. That this first part of the sequence moves to dawn, the last to dusk—however disjointed the in-between—has importance to me.

*This essay was written while I was in residence, as a Rockefeller Foundation Fellow to complete my *Collected Poems 1953–1983*, at the Bellagio Center in Italy.

The assumption of the poem's first part, then, is that it is possible through meditation to transform one's world. The difference between the occasional epiphany, however startling, of Western experience—defined and justly considered by James Joyce in *Portrait of the Artist as a Young Man*—and Zen *satori* of the depth realized by Hakuin is, put simply, that the passing of the epiphanic moment (a return to reality rather like the street stepped back into after a luminous few hours in a theater) is invariably a come-down, whereas true satori is permanent in its effects: the world (that street) has been forever altered. I would not claim to have experienced satori. In Zen one cannot make such claims—only a master is qualified to judge—yet the experience was more than epiphany: something profound was grasped, had its effect upon my life. It has lasted, grows in strength each time in imagination I return to it.

That is very personal, only one way of putting it, possibly even misleading, for Zen insists the world, perfect just as is, needs no tranformation. Rather it is we who must change our relationship to it—in effect, it is we who must undergo change, eyes seeing freshly. Thus responsibility is fully personal: no one to blame or praise, no condition to despair over, find fortunate, just the sudden (it is always that) awareness of where fault (answer) lies. It is never less than astonishing to regain the fullness of one's reality, to return to what we've ignored, possibly despised, and discover it marvelous. The last lines of the poem's first part attempt to express that recognition.

II

Zenkan is meditation through close observation, leading sometimes to startling awareness. In the poem's second part such quality of perception is suggested by ''ice flowers.'' There is also associative process: a vision of the glacier leads rapidly (transitional leap) to thought of a moment in one of Hakuin's remarkable satori descriptions here modified in verse. In the last tercet there is profound identification with the master. Mind points like a torch because there is hope of escaping, by whatever means, the icefield, i.e., the frozen condition of one's life.

As process zenkan is obviously not unique to Zen, or for that matter to religious experience, yet it is practiced by all Zen artists, possibly accounting in large measure for the sharp particularity of their work, from ink painting to haiku. Deep, clean seeing, fully expressed, can say much, as in this haiku by Basho:

> Snowy morning—
> one crow
> after another.

The poet does not feel called upon to explain that one is more keenly aware of the crow in snow, to the point of "crow-viewing."

Emergence from the "glacier's side" of a meadow suggests perhaps hope (sign?) of awakening, which is of course the goal of meditation. At this moment of fire and ice, pure transparency, the meditator comes face to face with his true self, cannot see in or beyond, and cannot move. Facing his condition, his "original self," as Zen defines, he may be on the way to altering his life.

III

By now the symbolic drift should be fairly clear, the gravity established. In this fragment the meditator closely observes another "device," this time a stone: slowly, as if a maker were examining a planet, with seasonal progression as the stone is turned, "spring to now." What follows might suggest rejection, by the stone, of such a role. It would seem that it is stone only, pure and simple, and like any other falling, raises a "small dust."

I have written elsewhere, in the introduction to *The Penguin Book of Zen Poetry,* of the danger to the Zenist of such "mentalization," as in this passage:

The Zen experience is centripetal, the artist's contemplation of subject sometimes referred to as "mind-pointing." The disciple in an early stage of discipline is asked to point the mind at (meditate upon) an object, say a bowl of water. At first he is quite naturally inclined to metaphorize, expand, rise imaginatively from water to lake, sea, clouds, rain. Natural, perhaps, but just the kind of "mentalization" Zen masters caution against. The disciple is instructed to continue until it is possible to remain strictly with the object, penetrating more deeply, no longer looking *at* it but, as the Sixth Patriarch Hui-neng maintained essential, *as* it. Only then will he attain the state of *muga,* so close an identification with object that the unstable mentalizing self disappears.

Why must we in order to value something imagine it larger, grander? Emptiness, in Zen, is what every thing *is,* alone, and what establishes *being* is context and relationship, as between the stone and hand that holds it, the eye that examines it—not what the mind transforms it to. To make such an image of stone is to rob it of its essential being, and ourselves of the greatest possible source of integrality, identification with real things of this world.

IV

This part concerns occasional awareness, always startling, that we name things inadequately, reductively, relieving ourselves of burdens of the unknown. It asks: is certainty necessary, or is it possible to feel—like Keats's ideal poet, possessed of "negative capability"—at ease with uncertainty? Zen meditation inevitably pulls toward such challenging, just as its formal "problems," *koans,* if seriously faced, may lead to great doubt concerning manners with which, hitherto, we explained reality to ourselves. The koan unties knots which have held the world together—rather it cuts them. We are set adrift by koan, forced to reexamine all, let the original man within us break free. The last lines of the piece suggest the meditator, uneasy at the prospect (''gathered breath''), ventures an answer, supplies a name. Just another name, as limiting as all the others have been, or one fully his own?

The Chinese master Ch'ing-yuan's famous saying may be appropriate:

> Before I had studied Zen I saw mountains as mountains, waters as waters. When I learned something of Zen, the mountains were no longer mountains, waters no longer waters. But now that I understand Zen, I am at peace with myself, seeing mountains once again as mountains, waters as waters.

And so may be this poem by the eighth-century Chinese poet Beirei:

> All Patriarchs are above our understanding,
> And they don't last forever.
> O my disciples, examine, examine.
> What? Why this. This only.

In a commentary on the poem in *Zen Poems of China and Japan: The Crane's Bill*, I write: ''The objection to 'learning' is that it inevitably leads to presuppositions concerning the nature of the world, a philosophy the creation of others, whereas meditation and the pure perception which must accompany it may lead to insight into the very nature of things, the world not yet 'created, conceptualized, made philosophy.' ''

It should be realized that the examination taking place in this part of ''Awakening'' is self-imposed, not a koan set by a master, that the meditator is so very far from Ch'ing-yuan's third stage, his doubts far from resolved.

V

This segment might suggest that long before there is consciousness of meditation's power, as with a child, it is in a sense used. Here, too, "device" has place. What astonished the meditator, the girl's father, was that her command was urgent, suddenly she seemed possessed by will to understand: suddenly, on a Lake Michigan beach, she had to be given a picture of the universe. It was she who thought of clasping hands, so as to define that universe. In writing this, the poet was reminded of the profound structurings of his childhood, arrived at through a similar process of meditation, especially when exposed to nature—trees, flowers, birds, stones, shells. Reminded of the self-created rituals, countings, touchings, all the secret ways which gave sense to his otherwise ruled world.

There is serious misunderstanding regarding Zen meditation. That it should be carried out, among fellow practitioners, in a *zendo*, that there should be, if only occasionally, the guidance of an authentic master, goes without saying. Yet unless the practice leads, slowly but surely, to new, permanent ways of dealing with reality, a constant state of meditation, it may be of little avail. Hakuin, most instructive of the great Rinzai masters, reveals to what degree he felt that meditation must be known by its fruits. Time and again he found it necessary, as the result of a strongly felt lapse, to return "to the mat" for prolonged sessions of *zazen*.

Hakuin was to insist, along with masters like Bankei-Eitaku, on the need to carry the meditative spirit out of the zendo into life. The meditative moment, we learn from such masters, is not special, something to be risen from, let alone descended into: it is every moment of full awareness, and can and should concern all. Children, at their best, well before learning to conduct their lives, do not discriminate between high, low, valuable, negligible. Simplest things, at the right moment, draw the deepest responses from them, become meditative devices. Surely it was in that sense Wordsworth understood the child to be father to the man.

VI

This snip of poem may appear to concern the process of de-creation, yet that was not the intention. The purpose was not to give dissolving body to Zen's first principle, that all passes, but to point at the relationship of all things, held together in the "gray sack" of air. It was also to image the essential form-lessness of all, in a world of illusory forms—flesh "between" skin and bone. As in the case of all Zen expression, the poem is a meditation on the nature of Void, in which all forms and individuating characteristics are stripped away. All is empty. Nowhere is this fundamental fact of Zen given fuller expression than in poetry of its masters.

It is also profoundly felt in prose of great meditators, such as Pingalaka, best known as commentator on Nagarjuna, the late second-century Buddhist dialectician whose writings were all-important to the formation of Zen. Pingalaka writes:

The cloth exists on account of the thread; the matting is possible on account of the rattan. If the thread had its own fixed, unchangeable self-essence, it could not be made out of the flax. If the cloth had its own fixed, unchangeable self-essence, it could not be made from the thread. But as in point of fact the cloth comes from the thread and the thread from the flax, it must be said that the thread as well as the cloth had no fixed, unchangeable self-essence. It is just like the relation that obtains between the burning and the burned. They are brought together under certain conditions, and thus there takes place a phenomenon called burning. The burning and the burned, each has no reality of its own. For when one is absent the other is put out of existence. It is so with all things in this world, they are all empty, without self, without absolute existence. They are like the will-o'-the-wisp.

It should not be necessary to comment on moral implica-
tions of such a view, yet not to maintain the living dimension
of Zen principles would be to do its practitioners an injustice.
Suffice it to say that if one holds such a view, one cannot be-
have aggressively. Such feelings have had powerful expres-
sion in the West, as at the beginning of D. H. Lawrence's
essay "We Need One Another":

> We lack peace because we are not whole. And we are not
> whole because we have known only a tithe of the vital rela-
> tionships we might have had. We live in an age which be-
> lieves in stripping away the relationships.

VII

The poem's conclusion offers something of a thematic sum-
mation: to one awakened, life in its fullness, beginning to
end, is not only bearable but joyous. The preference for
"dusk-light," the moment before day's (life's) end, suggests
the profoundest segment of light's cycle, when meditation is
most natural. Like the trees, man should release into the
"wash of darkness," fully aware of what acceptance means.

It is one of the world's paradoxes that he who loves life
most least fears its conclusion, yet there are few who attain
such a state of acceptance. For the very religious especially
there are needs of assurance of another chance, a further op-
portunity, miraculously in flesh. Karma, as real in Zen as in all
Buddhism, does not offer comfort of-bodily return. Perhaps
the most helpful analogy is of a candle which, before expiring,
passes its flame to another. The candle remains, only the
flame endures. In man's most luminous relationships with
things of earth, including one's fellows, there can be a sense
of profound exchanges, a passing on of the flame.

Perhaps the truest thing I can say about "Awakening" is
that throughout its making I was struggling to find my way to
clarity. Now, as I write these last few words the bells peal

again in the square below. Along the lake path to the church of San Giacomo comes a young bride clinging to her father's arm. They mount the steps, enter the door, and I can picture them moving past Perugino's great painting *The Deposition*, then down the aisle. Soon father will pass daughter, like a flame, on to another, and stand back as she goes on toward her new life.

ROBERT PENN WARREN

Recollection Long Ago: Sad Music

In Tennessee once the heart of the campfire glowed
With steady joy in its semi-globe
Defined by the high-arched nave of oaks against
Light-years of stars and the
Last scream space makes beyond space. Faces,

Encircling, in grave bemusement, leaned, and shadow
Played over the glint of eyes, eyes fixed
On the fingers white in their delicate dance
On strings of the box. And delicate
Was the melancholy that swelled each heart, and timed
The pulse in wrist, and wrist, and wrist—all while
The face leaned over the box
In shadow of hair that in firelight down-gleamed,
Smoother than varnish, and black. And like
A silver vine that upward to darkness twines,
The voice confirmed the sweet sadness
Young hearts gave us no right to.

No right to, yet. Though someday would,
As Time unveiled,
In its own dancing parody of grace,
The bony essence of each joke on joke.

But even back then perhaps we knew the dancing
Fingers enacted a truth past the pain declared
By that voice that somehow made pain sweet.

Would it be better or worse, if now
I could name the names I've lost, and see,
Virile or beautiful, those who, entranced, leaned?
I wish I knew what wisdom they had learned there.

The singer—her name it flees the fastest.
If only she'd toss back that varnished black screen
And let
Flame reveal cheek-curve, eye-shine.
To tell me her name.

Even now.

Some Comments

This poem, "Recollection Long Ago: Sad Music," is literally a recollection. I find that many poems have a germ in a recollection, but this is as literal, even in detail, as recollection permits after some three score years have done their work. One of the great puzzles of writing poetry over a long span of years is to decide—no, guess—why some small thing keeps coming back into memory, with more and more urgency that it be seen and heard. The question that underlies all such cases is, simply put: what is the difference between the fact (recollected) and the meaning (which grows, or may grow, into a poem)? Of course, poems of such long gestation really share in the process of all poems: the conversion of fact (real or imaginary) into meaning. But the long time required for the remembered fact to demand meaning makes some sort of difference.

The outlines of the basic episode, the basic "fact," come clear enough to me. The scene is an evening picnic of college in a distant woodland. But I don't even remember how I—an inexperienced and rather friendless freshman of sixteen, with only a month or so of college life behind me—ever got invited. Some older and wiser lad had leaned from his height and asked me. After the beer, or secretly passed white mule, after the gorging and horseplay and jokes, things quieted down somewhat. Night had settled down.

After a moment of silence a girl leaned over her box in the firelight and struck a first chord. Then, slowly, she began to sing, as her long, white fingers moved over the strings—singing some sad folk ballad of love and tragedy. I do not remember what ballad. But I do remember the silence that, after the horseplay and jokes and drinks, suddenly fell.

It was a very sad song, and in the new silence, a strange silence, all eyes were fixed on the dancing white fingers—

273

whiter than white against the hanging screen of black hair that cut off my view of her face. The words, of love betrayed, of bloodshed, are gone from me now, but the fingers danced as though in joy. I did not think of the joy then. The thought came long after, as the recollection took shape in imagination.

When did that happen? That night before I fell asleep under my army blanket? A month later, a year? Or years? But I do remember the strange hypnosis that engulfed the whole gang of erstwhile merrymakers. The event touched some strange depth in all.

As for the girl with the screen of glossy black hair and the white dancing fingers that made music out of some grim old reality, she filled my imagination. I never met her. She was definitely older than I, probably a junior or senior of twenty or more. When I did happen to see her, she seemed to have an awesome beauty. She wasn't just an ordinary, fresh-faced co-ed. But some of the magic of the picnic scene, the white fingers evoking tragedy into music and hypnosis, lingered about her—though God knows I never had the slightest interest in music. I saw her only a few fleeting times on the campus, and followed her for, say, fifty years, never sure that I could recognize the real face. But I never spoke to her. Not a word. I may have known her name—I *must* have found that out, or did I?—but I have long since forgotten it.

The recollection kept on recurring, with its not understandable meaning. The white fingers dancing in firelight, under the shadow of great oaks and the gloss of the concealing curtain of black hair, began to assume, faintly at first, a meaning. Not phrased at all for years. Not phrased, in fact, until I had the impulse to write the poem, and then the meaning simply grew out of the act of brooding reconstruction, this after all the years. The mystery lay in the question of how the dancing fingers made a hypnotic music out of the grief or tragedy of the ballad's story.

So finally, after all the years, the impulse struck me to write the poem, and with the vision before my eyes, in broad daylight, the poem began. As the lines got put down—scratched out, rewritten—another "meaning," or feeling (what in the end is the difference?), grew that had not occurred to me before, though even now unverbalized. I'll try to put it down now. From the dancing fingers, the music—all the things we call art or poetry, or even the poetry of the unworded mind— must spring from the brevity, defeat, and tragedy of life, once those strings are touched by the white fingers.

And I can't remember the name of the girl whose fingers touched those strings.

THEODORE WEISS

The Death of Fathers

Rummaging inside yourself
for clues and coming up
with nothing more than old
familiar news, you think
you have it hard.
                        Your
father having died when you
were still a child, you keep,
it's true, but faded sense
of him.
            Nearly as bad,
not long after that
the village he was born
and lived in all his life
dispersed.
                And now, as if
it joined, he with it,
the lost tribes of Virginia,
it survives, name only,
on discarded maps.
                        And you
blame blustering Pittsburgh,
the smoke of it, the noise
its days cannot contain,
the ruins it labors at.

But though my father died
when I was some years older,
I know, beyond all ordinary
disappearings, nothing
of his past, his country

(Hungary he called it,
a few oaths still peppery
on my tongue what's left
to prove it), least of all
his town.
              New vandals
rampant, kicking boundaries
about, entire nations on
the run, as though their
lands were made of wind-

blown sand, how expect
to know? Like you I try
to ferret out some hints
of him from the one source
still available—myself.

Recall a few of his
loved saws like "The apple
falls not far from its tree."
But only a worm sticks
its fat tongue out at me.

Or "Teddy, I understand
you all right. Are you not
my son?" Well, was he not
my father? Clues or not,
I plunge into my writing,

chase fast scribbled
line on line, lean hard
on his robustious love:
his skill with animals:
his pleasure in the violin

he played by ear, gypsy
gaiety, abandon, gathered
up like grapes ripening

within his fingers' will:
his passion for his work,

my awe at watching him
delight in old things, new,
he bought to sell, green
cabinets he danced among,
as he, a young boy then,

shoes astride his neck,.
had skipped along (he told
me this?) the speckled path
dividing the Black Forest:
pride that almost drove

him, raging, over cliffs
and finally, when he would,
despite strong warnings,
mount a frisky horse, rode
him off forever,
      I there
as he stumbles up, eyes
closed, face set, the iron
bar lying just behind him
for what it's done
       moved
little farther than before,
a last cry, mother's name,
still hot upon his lips.
He staggered about,

I, gripping his arm,
summon all my strength
("Am I not your son?"
Surely I can reach him,
haul him back) to learn—

as I shout ''Father!''
over the growing chasm,
his breath slammed shut,
a wall instantly gone up—
the lesson never learned.

The Fruits of Loss

Poets often admit, with something like a parental sense of surprise, pride, pleasure, that once a poem is finished it becomes someone else's, becomes someone else. In fact, it must do so to constitute a free-standing, independent work. Thus the poet's comments and recollections may be no more relevant or trustworthy than anyone else's. As Lawrence has said, the reader should trust the poem rather than its maker's account of it. What does one remember, especially after a deal of living has intervened, of a war-torn past, a complicated love affair so engrossing one had all one could do to survive, let alone observe? For in writing a poem when the going is good (or bad), the poet's self, its consciousness, not so much dissolves or is abeyant, but, totally busy, so submerged, becomes, with the poet's other faculties, pure act.

Like others, I am chary about remarks on what I have written. I know the whimsicality, the mischievousness, of memory. If the truth be told, I usually prefer to wipe out all traces and to scatter whatever scaffolding I may have opportunistically employed in the catch-as-catch-can of composing. As poets cheerfully (or defiantly) insist, the poem is what it is. If you do not understand it or fully take it in the first time (Why should you? Why expect to? Not if the poet respects you and your past, your experience. During a first visit to a bustling city, can you take in all its activities, master it and its layout perfectly?), like Frost I suggest that the best explanation for the poem is reading it again. Obviously if I had needed all this essay's words I would have included them in the poem.

However, to the extent that poets have become public readers, even considerable performers, they have grown accustomed to commenting on their own work, to providing contexts, anecdotes, observations for involving the hearer. At times, in fact, some poets are more striking, if not more poetic, in their commentary than in their poems, so that one is tempted to ask: "Why instead of the poem didn't you write that? Or why at least didn't you get it into the poem?" In any case, in the democracy of criticism poets should enjoy as much suffrage, sufferance too, as anyone else. Furthermore, some special interest may derive out of what has happened in the poet's mind anent his poem since it was written. Poems are a kind of palimpsest, with many buried cities in and behind them, cities still lively if the poet is lucky. He may have access to, may be able to highlight some of those cities. He may even be amused to remark, like the jokes and puns Joyce planted in his work for his own pleasure, shades of meaning, allusions, private resources only he can know. At least that is what the following pages would be up to.

As this poem and this essay propose, it may be wise for us now to be less impatient with the past and what it has to tell us. For through much of our history we Americans have faced resolutely westward and futureward. The Old World's dust dropped behind, we have proudly dismissed thoughts of the past, even our own. We could, we believed, jettison all the mistakes, crimes, shames of that past and, like Adam, with no memory, unless it be of God and creation itself, start over. Each new migration, whatever its source, has repeated this attitude. One can sympathize with a good measure of it. Many immigrants have had, beyond poverty, hardship, or persecution, not too much to remember and a great deal to forget. For a number of these, had they remained in Europe, aside from the vast slaughter of the two World Wars, the Nazis, seeing to a consummation of their conditions, would have cleansed them of memory altogether.

My father, a young Hungarian arrived in the United States, having fled his country's compulsory military service, promptly became a 237% American, overwhelmedly grateful for its freedoms, its promises: there seemed to be no limit to what he might do, to how high he might go. Add to that sentiment constant mobility (in my father's restlessness we, like countless other Americans, emulated the early nomadic tribes—not flocks and grazing but jobs and business took us wherever they would), and the past seemed entirely obliterated. My father almost never mentioned his past; and since my mother was Philadelphia-born, except for occasional conversations with some of his countrymen, his language and his country failed to enter my early consciousness. Until fully grown, and then too late because of his death and the death of all his relatives, I never thought to look into his past. Once I began to write poetry, Europe, its culture and history, amply filled my thoughts. But Europe with its past as a living place was, in my plunge into the present, of even less interest to me than my own earliest days. When I learned of Stevens's passion for his ancestors I was amazed. It struck me, in one so sophisticated and intelligent, as odd, even ridiculous, if not entirely irrelevant.

My wife's and my first trip to Europe, however, one I undertook reluctantly (what, beyond its books and arts which I thought I already knew, could it tell me worth knowing, worth taking time from my own busy, full-time present?), and then a year in England did much to shake my indifference, my provinciality. First of all, to my astonishment and often to my irritation, I found my being an American willy-nilly thrust upon me. Before challenging questions I became defensive, if not—especially since this response was at times exacted of me: as one Englishman sneered at me, "Beyond that chap, Poe is it, have you any poets?"—offensive. I returned from Europe with sentiments not far from those in my "Ruins for these Times":

> To hell with holy relics,
> sniffing like some mangy dog
> after old, dead scents (saints?),
> those that went this way before
> and went. More shambling about
> in abandoned, clammy churches
> and I abjure all religion,
> even my own!

(I did not realize then how much shambling about I would be involved in later in my long poem *Recoveries*!) The poem eventually says,

> What's the mess of Europe,
> late or antique, great or antic,
> to the likes of me?

Yet, for all my bravado, I was stung. During our English year in Iffley, a tiny suburb of Oxford, sharing a house with an old Scottish woman, Mrs. Collingwood, the widow of a famous Oxford don, I especially felt troubled. Though she became a dear friend, at the same time she

>   . . . regards you
> incredulously, a bastard gargoyle
> off some bastard architecture,
> one that simply grew:
>   'Not to know
> your great-grandfather! How do
> you live? O you Americans!'

In truth, though my mother's parents, who lived with us for a considerable time, were close, I did not know my father's parents, let alone theirs; what's worse, I knew nothing about them, not even their names. Of course I usually shrugged off Mrs. C.'s attitude as mere antiquarianism. So the poem responds,

>   She
> cannot see what freedom it affords,
> your ignorance,
>   a space swept
> clear of all the clutter of lives
> lived.

But she had reached me, for the poem admits,

> And yet who can dismiss
> her words entirely? It burdens too
> this emptiness,
>   a massive presence
> not a room away that, no matter
> how you hammer at its wall,
> refuses to admit you.

I cite early poems because, as anyone who has written a good deal knows, when we write what we think is at last new, not only does it usually turn out on second look to be close kin to old poems, but many poems are, wittingly or not, rehearsals for later ones. Not that the earlier poems were necessarily dry runs since they fulfilled themselves by getting to wherever they were going (sometimes with luck even farther!), but, whatever their self-sufficiency, they can be important way stations to a final grappling with a situation fundamental to the poet.

At the same time poets often find it embarrassing—at least they used to—if not impossible, to write directly about those very near to them. Where is the distance, the objectivity, the freedom of treatment to come from? And who wants to reveal—so risk losing—precious, private details? But the poet can try to get at such relations obliquely, by dressing them in historical or fabulous characters like Oedipus or Cleopatra. That way the poet can feel free to fill those stand-ins with his or her thoughts and feelings, even the most intimate. Moreover, such substitutes encourage greater range. Recently, however, with Freud and the couch, with the invitation from television and the other media to all-out confession, and with the appetite, never greater than now, for gossip, the hunger people have (out of loneliness, frustration, lives blocked?) for other lives, poets have felt easier about moving into self-declaration.

I have often struggled with this problem. Confession, expressing publicly the most secret details of myself, has never particularly appealed to me. Yet I have wished to dip into the special wells of feeling my parents sprang in me, the first wells and in some ways the deepest and purest. The present poem's title is fairly neutral, if not opaque. It needs its poem for meaning. A commonplace, it derives from King Claudius's bluff speech in *Hamlet*. I chose it not so much for certification, profit by association, literary company with the great, as for suggesting a universal context, for a sense of the bafflement of each human being before a basic, "ordinary," inevitable event: our bafflement before death through one most dear. The title, in its admission of loss, links that loss to the world at large.

What prompted the poem or at least made it possible was my being able to find company in another who had already expressed a similar frustration—ignorance before his origins. That complaint and regret supplied a scaffolding and a place for me to stand and to take off from, a place for fellow-feeling, argument, challenge. An argument with another that enables me to get my argument with myself out into the open. The other had, like me, in last resort attempted one of the poet's basic enterprises: digging into the self. If the outside world will not help, will not afford the longed-for information of facts, the precious details, of personal history, then we must try memory, probe the recesses of our own beings with their living ties to the past, stored in them like a hive, for the honey of origins. As one of the Seven Wise Men said, "Omnia mea me cum porto": All that is mine I carry with me.

The person referred to here had lost in childhood, in addition to his father, the village his father had all his life been identified with and, as in a living, life-sized map, written out all his living in. That place, dispersed like so much smoke, was left at best in markings on early maps; and through later developments, the ravaging life of the city, it was lost even more. In the childlike competitiveness we are given to, one that suggests a self-assurance even able to derive pleasure, if not pride, from its greater deprivations and inferiorities, I almost boast that, if the first one has lost his father and his town as well, I have not even useless maps or the certain name of my father's country, let alone his town. My father's past—as if he were indeed a victim of the Nazis with their methodical annihilation of a person beyond his body by way of his name and any record of him—has disappeared as though it had never existed. My grief before this fact is strengthened by a sense of shame, of guilt, for not remembering. In being cavalier, if not indifferent, had I not, in my own way, been as destructive as the Nazis?

The name of the country my father claimed as his own still reverberates on the air a moment, commingled with the few mouth-filling oaths, spicy as that country's dishes, I had overheard and remember. And now and then repeat as though they might, attaching to other words, draw in whole sentences, their seasons round them, scenes and people: might like a magician's spell conjure up the whole lost world. But for what the age at large has done, immeasurably more efficient than the other's Pittsburgh, all I have is a chaotic world and an unanswerable question—namely, whether the Hungary my father claimed is Hungary now or, for wars and invasions, some submerged part of another country. Not till the dismal, icy, winter nights when, bent over the radio, my father and I together heard of Hitler's steady, speedy advance like an ungainsayable glacier over all Europe, especially when Hungary itself was in danger and then engulfed, did I finally, despite the nothing said, feel something of my father's Europeanism, his concern for his native country.

Brought up against the ragged edges of this void, I resort to the other's stratagem: a plumbing of the self, the memory. If the original language and landscape cannot be tapped, perhaps something of my father can be summoned through a few of his favorite old sayings. Maybe something more will cling to them, in their echoing a larger music. But this would-be ritual mainly results in mockery, the worm licking its chops mid-feast, the dead end of an all-knowing rather than self-revealing father. Desperately I take to the one course I have spent much of my life on—headlong writing. Perhaps, faithfully followed (I put down words and then I follow them), it will not only chart the desired route but finally uncover the hoped-for treasure. For landmarks, the verses lean on, as they lasso, those traits of my father's which I most cherishingly remember.

In short order these landmarks are raced through to suggest their happening together and together composing a whole man. They are to suggest the various vitality I hope will inform the lines; perhaps, like the *Hamlet* ghost, my father can be conjured up to tell his story. Briefly he does seem present, in activities I had described in earlier poems and interviews. (So in "Ruins for these Times":

> a father
> who keeps coming apart however
> I try to patch him together
> again. Old age too much for him,
> the slowly being picked to pieces
> as a boy with a fly, he hopped
> a spunky horse and left
> change gaping in the dust.)

Chief among these traits was my father's voluble affection, out of which all the other memories stem, an affection given to great demonstrativeness in private and out. Then I recall my father's need to keep animals near him, near the many stores—five-and-tens, department stores, shoe stores, secondhand stores—he restlessly opened and abandoned. There he bred pheasants, rare pigeons, rare fowl he would watch by the hour. A little chick-pheasant, born with a crooked, nonsupporting leg, he saved by attaching that leg to a splint he carved. So he saved a nest of eggs, when its mother was run over by a car, making another hen drunk so that, grown sober, she sat on that nest as her own. Or he lined the whole partitioned-off back wall of his shoe store in the town's main street with cage upon cage of canaries.

Next the violin which my father, by listening to gypsies, had taught himself so that he could whip off some lively folk tunes (the violin he loved so much he did everything he could to persuade me to master it, even hiring a young man to practice with me). And then, part and parcel of my father's gusto, his passionate absorption—it swallowed up most of his days and a good part of his nights as well—in buying and selling anything and everything, from new filing cabinets (which I, home from graduate school, had watched him in awing, sheer pleasure cavort around as he pointed them out in his musty

warehouse) to silk-mill machines, to used desks and refrigera-
tors, to buildings. Or as I like to say, ''If he caught you stand-
ing absentmindedly on a street corner, he'd sell you too!''

These cabinets, for the glossy-green pastorality they sug-
gest, swing me to one of the very few memories I have of my
father's past: his walking through the famous Black Forest, al-
ways to me, for its name alone and the almost nothing I know
of it, a place of enchantment, tantalizing fright, a haunt of
sylphs, wolves, Dracula. Striding through the forest, fast on
my father's lost footsteps, I come to my father's fury, rages I
called on as a child when, attacked by other schoolboys, I,
running home, at the top of my house's steps would shout:
''You better watch out or I'll get my father's Hungarian fits!''
My father's rage was never better than when my mother com-
plained in the car how much more—a fur coat, jewels, new
furniture, a vacation—some other wife had than she. My fa-
ther, storming, would offer to drive the car over the cliff, just
stopping at the edge.

Still occupied with my father's love for animals and his as-
sumption of mastery over them, I recall one day when I and
my wife were visiting my home. My father took us and my
mother out to the farm of one of his customers, a place he es-
pecially liked for its animals. With the lure of riding he urged
us to accompany him. While our party was in the owner's
house, my father left, no doubt to exhibit his horsemanship
by cantering by. Forgetting how long it had been since he had
last ridden, he led a horse out of the stable and sought to
mount it. Almost instantly it must have thrown him. At that
moment I, for whatever reason, felt called on to investigate,
and I came on him just as he rose, staggered about for a mo-
ment, then, with his wife's name his last breath, fell dead to
the ground. A large iron bar nearby was probably what had
struck his head. It seemed sadly appropriate that he, who had
said to me, ''Teddy, I can't take this getting old''; he always
on the restless go, as in our moving about in a fairly tight circle
from one little town to another—Allentown, Pennsylvania,
that moving's hub always returned to; he who drove his
many cars like mettlesome horses, soon wearing them out,
should mount a horse that carried him off. It is as though he

chose time's winged chariot and being flung from it at once rather than endure its dragging him ignominiously at its wheels in the dust. In a sense, what he lived by he died by.

At this juncture, recapitulating the poem's ambition, I seek to hold on to my father. In fine, I resort to the same ruse of energy I hoped would help me write this poem. But, on the contrary, with every breath my father is farther away. The apple may not fall far from the tree, and in itself it may sum up all that tree and its past. Yet how shall it cover the brief, vast distance to climb back onto its original bough and feel that tree's life from its far-off roots, especially if the tree be felled? Here I learn the lesson the poem has been fumbling toward, the unbridgeable gap between even related, loving individuals. Ironically enough, my father for all his vigor and assertive love leaves behind only so much cogent silence. This accident has brought us up against an unbudgeable reality—the lasting knowledge of our abysmal, abiding ignorance.

So the writing of the last verse itself has proved most difficult. In its first printed form it was "the fundamental lesson," which would mean that what we learn most of all is that separate we are, a mystery to each other, and separate we must be. Since then, after many variations, the line has become "the lesson never learned." For what is being taught is that we cannot learn, can never learn to accept, what the poem has illustrated. My father, a moment ago an emphatic presence, has unbelievably gone, turned into a thing, a stone, like the bar that may have catapulted him over the impenetrable, final barrier. At last I enjoy the terrible, ripened fruits of my and my father's wish: we are indeed Americanly complete, cut off, not only from Europe and the past, but from each other and, in a fundamental sense, from ourselves. At least suggested here is the acknowledgment, if not acceptance, of our limits and our limitations and an acknowledgment of, if not submission to, the all that we are not, the infinite we reach only by not being. Or a knowledge we cannot know, that would deny us even our death as it denies—fails to recognize—our life. The details and the individuals we clutch in the hope that they will clutch us must let go, and finally we embrace the other as it wholly embraces us. Yet till the end we recoil from the very knowledge we lust after.

The short, getting-on-with-it verse of the poem sprang from its initial impulse, the urgency of the poem's quest. As die, falling, call their number, so the first lines established their metrical number. Once the basic breath is discovered it blossoms out into the unique shape the poem must take. So the rhythm is settled, the line breaks, the voicing and pacing; and the stanza units, each thought-and-feeling accommodated by five lines, are fairly contained until the break prompted by the age's chaos, hesitated over in "lands were made of wind-." Wind they have become for the turmoil they and their peoples have been subjected to. Again, a running on occurs in and after "I plunge into my writing" and in the verses enumerating the speaker's father's traits, until the last stanzas when the final, chaotic drama takes over, the accident and the face set (against the speaker) like "iron." From such lean lines we hang, yet learn the truth that, as we receive life and living from our fathers, so we receive and are instructed in death through them.

RICHARD WILBUR

Lying

To claim, at a dead party, to have spotted a grackle,
When in fact you haven't of late, can do no harm.
Your reputation for saying things of interest
Will not be marred, if you hasten to other topics,
Nor will the delicate web of human trust
Be ruptured by that airy fabrication.
Later, however, talking with toxic zest
Of golf, or taxes, or the rest of it
Where the beaked ladle plies the chuckling ice,
You may enjoy a chill of severance, hearing
Above your head the shrug of unreal wings.
Not that the world is tiresome in itself:
We know what boredom is: it is a dull
Impatience or a fierce velleity,
A champing wish, stalled by our lassitude,
To make or do. In the strict sense, of course,
We invent nothing, merely bearing witness
To what each morning brings again to light:
Gold crosses, cornices, astonishment
Of panes, the turbine-vent which natural law
Spins on the grill-end of the diner's roof,
Then grass and grackles or, at the end of town
In sheen-swept pastureland, the horse's neck
Clothed with its usual thunder, and the stones
Beginning now to tug their shadows in
And track the air with glitter. All these things
Are there before us; there before we look
Or fail to look; there to be seen or not
By us, as by the bee's twelve thousand eyes,
According to our means and purposes.
So too with strangeness not to be ignored,
Total eclipse or snow upon the rose,

And so with that most rare conception, nothing.
What is it, after all, but something missed?
It is the water of a dried-up well
Gone to assail the cliffs of Labrador.
There is what galled the arch-negator, sprung
From Hell to probe with intellectual sight
The cells and heavens of a given world
Which he could take but as another prison:
Small wonder that, pretending not to be,
He drifted through the bar-like boles of Eden
In a *black mist low creeping,* dragging down
And darkening with moody self-absorption
What, when he left it, lifted and, if seen
From the sun's vantage, seethed with vaulting hues.
Closer to making than the deftest fraud
Is seeing how the catbird's tail was made
To counterpoise, on the mock-orange spray,
Its light, up-tilted spine; or, lighter still,
How the shucked tunic of an onion, brushed
To one side on a backlit chopping-board
And rocked by trifling currents, prints and prints
Its bright, ribbed shadow like a flapping sail.
Odd that a thing is most itself when likened:
The eye mists over, basil hints of clove,
The river glazes toward the dam and spills
To the drubbed rocks below its crashing cullet,
And in the barnyard near the sawdust-pile
Some great thing is tormented. Either it is
A tarp torn loose and in the groaning wind
Now puffed, now flattened, or a hip-shot beast
Which tries again, and once again, to rise.
What, though for pain there is no other word,
Finds pleasure in the cruellest simile?
It is something in us like the catbird's song
From neighbor bushes in the grey of morning
That, harsh or sweet, and of its own accord,
Proclaims its many kin. It is a chant
Of the first springs, and it is tributary
To the great lies told with the eyes half-shut

That have the truth in view: the tale of Chiron
Who, with sage head, wild heart, and planted hoof
Instructed brute Achilles in the lyre,
Or of the garden where we first mislaid
Simplicity of wish and will, forgetting
Out of what cognate splendor all things came
To take their scattering names; and nonetheless
That matter of a baggage-train surprised
By a few Gascons in the Pyrenees—
Which, having worked three centuries and more
In the dark caves of France, poured out at last
The blood of Roland, who to Charles his king
And to the dove that hatched the dovetailed world
Was faithful unto death, and shamed the Devil.

Some Notes on "Lying"

I

Back in the late 1940s, just after World War II, one of my closest Cambridge friends was André du Bouchet, who had come to America as a refugee, studied at Amherst and Harvard, and would soon go back to France to become one of its leading poets. Then, as young men in our twenties, we were quite besotted with poetry, writing it constantly, continually theorizing about it, and translating each other's work. Oddly enough, though we were both earnestly engaged in leftist politics, we were attracted in theory (for a time at least) toward a poetry which should be pure, disrelated, autotelic. André introduced me to Villiers de l'Isle-Adam ("Vivre? Nos valets le feront pour nous"), and I made a translation of Villiers's *Claire Lenoir*. And then there was the example of Raymond Roussel's *Impressions d'Afrique*, which (as I remember) based its fictions upon meaningless puns such as *vers/vers*, and thus achieved a near-perfect impertinence to the world. On one occasion André observed that it would be a pure creative act to announce that one had seen a squirrel in front of the Fogg Museum, if one had *not* seen a squirrel there; one would thus harmlessly and disinterestedly introduce into the minds of one's friends a squirrel which had never existed.

Not long ago, I was fascinated to find, in a memoir of Dylan Thomas by one of his boyhood friends, that the young Thomas had entertained a similar notion. It seemed to him a poetic act to inform his mother that he was carrying a handkerchief in his right-hand pocket, whereas in fact the handkerchief was in his *left*-hand pocket.

My poem "Lying" is not an indictment of du Bouchet and Thomas, whose early aesthetic ideas, like mine, could be briefly, airily, and somewhat jocularly held. But I do owe to them my unreal grackle. It occurred to me (apparently) that a

301

poem about truth and poetry might well start obliquely with a piddling and ludicrous instance of fraudulent "creation," and then proceed to take its implications seriously. It is a fundamental impulse of poetry to refresh the aspect of things. The Dada movement was a mockery and subversion of certain worn-out attitudes toward reality; the unreal-grackle theory of poetry partakes of the same impatience with stale formulations, but it is more extreme and it threatens to touch the thought of even the soberest poet. Because poetry can so charge and heighten the world in language; because it can approach sheer incantation, as in "Pale, beyond porch and portal"; because it can say things like "A deed without a name"; because, when it speaks of "the barren Plains / Of *Sericana,* where *Chineses* drive / With Sails and Wind thir cany Waggons light," we are given at least as much magic as information, the poet is prone to the illusion that he can make or unmake the world, or create an alternative reality. This he cannot do, and in proportion as he is touched by that illusion he confesses a timidity about doing what he *can* do—interact with the given world, see and feel and order it newly. W. J. Turner begins a wild and remarkable poem with the line "In despair at being unable to rival the creations of God." It is perhaps because everybody is something of a poet, and can understand that line, that I addressed my poem to "You."

II

I think I knew from the beginning that Milton's Satan would get into my poem, because the illusory aesthetic of which I've been speaking is ultimately Satanic. Satan, in his insanity, sets himself up as a rival to the Creator, but he can make nothing, and is capable at most of parodies, impostures, and temporary destructions. Did I choose blank verse because I glimpsed Milton in the offing? I suspect that I was more influenced by the fact that pentameter is the most flexible of our meters, and the best in which to build large verse-masses; I must have sensed that, though the drift of the poem would finally be simple, I would wish to deal fluently and amply with the sensible richness of things, and with the world as a dense tissue of resemblances.

The poem assumes that the essential poetic act is the discovery of resemblance, the making of metaphor, and that, the world being one thing, all metaphor tends toward the truth.

III

"Lying," because it is urging the unity of things, expresses the idea not only by near comparisons and far linkages, but also by a certain velocity—by quick shifts and transitions. Does that make sense? I know, for example, that "and nonetheless," in the eighth line from the end, is very sudden and condensed. I leave it to the reader to decide whether all my rapid jumps and splices help to enforce the meaning or not.

What I'm sure of is that a high subject, unless perhaps one is writing a hymn, should not be approached with remorseless nobility, and this poem has its comic elements, as many of mine do. Comedy is serious; it is the voice of balance; and its presence in a serious poem is a test and earnest of its earnestness. One wants anything of moment to be said by the whole self in all its languages. Thus one also includes everyday locutions ("What is it, after all . . ."), ordinary words like "shucked," ordinary things like chopped onions.

IV

More than one reader has said to me that the phrase "Some great thing is tormented" is crucial to the poem, and I agree. The argument had to embrace not only "nature" but also turbine-vents and tarps. It also had to acknowledge suffering as part of the fabric of life, as it does by seeing or imagining a big Holstein with a hopelessly dislocated hip. The catbird, who sings of the kinship of things, sings even of this, though harshly, because the kinship outweighs the suffering. So say I, at any rate.

V

When I first showed "Lying" to my wife, who is always the first and best reader of my poems, she said, "Well, you've finally done it; you've managed to write a poem that's incomprehensible from beginning to end." Then, reading it again, she came to find it, considered as a statement, quite forthright. It seems that "Lying" is the sort of poem which ought first to be heard or read without any distracting anxiety to catch all of its connections and local effects, and that it then asks to be absorbed in several readings or hearings. I make no apology for that: some of the poetry written these days has the relaxed transparency of talk, and would not profit by being mulled over, but much is of the concentrated kind which closes with an implicit *da capo*. Provided it's any good, a poem which took months to write deserves an ungrudging quarter hour from the reader.

I find, in making these notes, that I'm reluctant to expound the obvious, saying for instance that there are "lies" or fictions which are ways of telling the truth, and that the poem ends with three fictions having one burden. What I would most respond to, in conversation with an interested reader, would be noticings or questionings of details: the use of birds throughout, and of the word "shrug" for the hovering of an unreal grackle; the echo of Job, and its intended evocation of a whole passage; the water-figure, strange but not untrue, in which the idea of "nothing" is dismissed; the transformation of the *black mist* into a rainbow; the perching of the catbird on a mock-orange spray; the vitrification of a river, beginning with "glazes" and ending with "cullet." But the fact is that the details are too many for me to worry them in this space; what we have here, I figure, is a baroque poem, in the sense that it is a busy and intricate contraption which issues in plainness.

C. K. WILLIAMS

From My Window

Spring: the first morning when that one true block of sweet,
    laminar, complex scent arrives
from somewhere west and I keep coming to lean on the sill,
    glorying in the end of the wretched winter.
The scabby-barked sycamores ringing the empty lot across the
    way are budded—I hadn't noticed—
and the thick spikes of the unlikely urban crocuses have al-
    ready broken the gritty soil.
Up the street, some surveyors with tripods are waving each
    other left and right the way they do.
A girl in a gym suit jogged by a while ago, some kids passed,
    playing hooky, I imagine,
and now the paraplegic Vietnam vet who lives in a half-
    converted warehouse down the block
and the friend who stays with him and seems to help him out
    come weaving towards me,
their battered wheelchair lurching uncertainly from one edge
    of the sidewalk to the other.
I know where they're going—to the "Legion": once, when I
    was putting something out, they stopped,
both drunk that time, too, both reeking—it wasn't ten o'clock
    —and we chatted for a bit.
I don't know how they stay alive—on benefits most likely. I
    wonder if they're lovers?
They don't look it. Right now, in fact, they look a wreck, ca-
    reening haphazardly along,
contriving, as they reach beneath me, to dip a wheel from the
    curb so that the chair skewers, teeters,
tips, and they both tumble, the one slowly, almost gracefully
    sliding in stages from his seat,
his expression hardly marking it, the other staggering over
    him, spinning heavily down,

307

to lie on the asphalt, his mouth working, his feet shoving
    weakly and fruitlessly against the curb.

In the storefront office on the corner, Reed and Son, Real Es-
    tate, have come to see the show.

Gazing through the golden letters of their name, they're not,
    at least, thank god, laughing.

Now the buddy, grabbing at a hydrant, gets himself erect and
    stands there for a moment, panting.

Now he has to lift the other one, who lies utterly still, a fore-
    arm shielding his eyes from the sun.

He hauls him partly upright, then hefts him almost all the
    way into the chair but a dangling foot

catches a support-plate, jerking everything around so that he
    has to put him down,

set the chair to rights and hoist him again and as he does he
    jerks the grimy jeans right off him.

No drawers, shrunken, blotchy thighs: under the thick, white
    coils of belly blubber,

the poor, blunt pud, tiny, terrified, retracted, is almost invisi-
    ble in the sparse genital hair,

then his friend pulls his pants up, he slumps wholly back as
    though he were, at last, to be let be,

and the friend leans against the cyclone fence, suddenly star-
    ing up at me as though he'd known,

all along, that I was watching and I can't help wondering if he
    knows that in the winter, too,

I watched, the night he went out to the lot and walked, paced
    rather, almost ran, for how many hours.

It was snowing, the city in that holy silence, the last we have,
    when the storm takes hold,

and he was making patterns that I thought at first were circles
    then realized made a figure eight,

what must have been to him a perfect symmetry but which,
    from where I was, shivered, bent,

and lay on its side: a warped, unclear infinity, slowly, as the
    snow came faster, going out.

Over and over again, his head lowered to the task, he slogged
    the path he'd blazed,

but the race was lost, his prints were filling faster than he
  made them now and I looked away,
up across the skeletal trees to the tall center city buildings,
  some, though it was midnight,
with all their offices still gleaming, their scarlet warning-
  beacons signalling erratically
against the thickening flakes, their smoldering auras soften-
  ing portions of the dim, milky sky.
In the morning, nothing: every trace of him effaced, all the
  field pure white,
its surface glittering, the dawn, glancing from its glaze, ob-
  lique, relentless, unadorned.

On "From My Window"

Usually my poems are very difficult for me to write. They seem to demand an enormous tension, or a series of tensions, usually over a period of months or years, before I can find what they were meaning to be and what form they were meant to take. Although when a poem is done, the work that went into it is always in some gratifying way reabsorbed into the concrete fact of its existence, my sense of composition is still generally one of strenuous willing. The few poems that come more easily, as did "From My Window," are intriguing to me, mostly because the labor they demanded seemed to have more to do with what was actually going on in the poem rather than in the overcoming of all the various character lapses and lacks that constitute so much of the act of writing, but also because there always seems to be a great deal in them I wasn't quite aware of bringing about.

Although the generating event of "From My Window"—the two men in the street—had happened three or four years before, when the memory of it came to me, I knew immediately that there would be a poem in it; the working out of the poem was relatively easy, and very exciting. It was as though the poem was already there for me; its existence, that existence which can sometimes seem so tenuous, depending on so many problematical acts of inspiration, was already assured. I felt as though I was *in* the poem somehow, wandering through it. My task was simply to note and to record, and all that was demanded of me was enough patience and attentiveness to find the proper music and figurations for the poem. I even intuited very clearly (and very uncharacteristically) what its rate of disclosure would be. Every day I would wait for whatever segment was to be, not revealed, because revealed implies something hidden or obscure, but rather given to me. It seemed that everything in the poem was already available: all my mind's eye had to do was focus, in this direction, then in that. Although, in fact, most of the other details and events in the poem are fictitious, or were dug up out of notebooks and the drafts of failed poems, their place in the mechanism, once I came across them, would immediately be self-evident. The men in the real-estate office, for instance, I found in something I'd tried (and am still trying) to write about wealth and love, and as soon as I had found them, it was as though they were already in the poem; all I had done was to glance up the street to notice them. My energy, instead of being devoted to searching for an element which would triangulate the exchanges between the veterans and the narrator, could go instead towards figuring those kabbalistic letters on the plate glass of their office, and to introducing into the poem, albeit in an ejaculation, divinity, that divinity which is always potential to our reflections.

All this happened—the writing of the poem—quite a while ago, five years or so. In reflecting on work that old, one imagines there'll be surprises, but perhaps because the poem did come so readily, I'm struck again by how much there is in it I wasn't entirely conscious of putting there. I know I'd meant the poem to be about forgetfulness, about sublimation, evasion, repression, false gestures of transcendence, false faith, loss of hope, and, in a deeper sense, about hope itself. Most of these clearly have to do with our relationships with time, but when I was working on the poem I'm quite sure I wasn't aware, as I am in looking at it now, of how many of the incidents and details are enactments or embodiments of those relations. The seasons, first of all, and how uncannily, almost biologically aware we are in our discernment of them; the young jogger, trying already to outrun age and death; the surveyors who measure and record for us, because our common memory is not to be trusted for such serious business as dividing up the planet; the warehouse, a receptacle against the trials of time which has itself become a victim of time, converted to less noble uses; the "Legion," that exercise in lost glory and an often fierce, vindictive, reactionary nostalgia. Even the fat on the paralytic's belly is an accumulation of his desperations, the friend's obsessive tramping in the night is the image of his, and that innocent figure eight, which figuratively becomes a segment of infinity-eternity, is possibly the symbol of our own.

If I don't remember quite how I came to all the detailing of the poem, nor even what made me recall that terribly tumbling wheelchair in the first place, I do remember very clearly what the impetus for writing the poem was. When I'd watched that morning from my study as the travail of the two men unfolded, I'd been very upset, taken aback, embarrassed for them, with that strangely acute unease we can feel for strangers who forget their lines, whose tragedies or griefs or rages flood over into our lives. As I watched it again, though, in my imagination now, most of that feeling was gone. There was very little perturbation; I felt detached instead, cool, professional. I was seeing, and seeking, auras, atmospheres. Then something shifted again and made me realize suddenly that what had been really crucial in my original response had somehow been coped with in my consciousness, de-dramatized, shriven of nearly all the discomfort I'd felt as it was happening. Furthermore, it was at that moment that I seemed to have to confront and to admit to myself that without my quite noticing, my experience of the whole Vietnam war had in some essential way also changed; it, too, had found a crease in my memory mechanisms; it no longer held for me the same rages of offended justice and rationality it had so recently.

But so what? Forgetfulness is one of the gods' most precious offerings to us. The war, after all, was over; there are certainly always examples enough to arouse our outrage at government's grim, obtuse conviction to repeat its errors and its crimes. Why be so upset about letting that wretched war just go?

It had something to do for me with a deep sense of incompletion. Nothing had happened in the public world to redeem the war, to make it in any sense an effective sort of object lesson. We would have Iran, we would have El Salvador and Nicaragua, as we had had Korea and Guatemala, but there was no comfort in that, because I understood that each of them in its turn would erode into the same spiritless channels of meaninglessness and futility, and it felt to me then as though all the fervor and passion that we had experienced, we who'd been against the war, the liberals and the radicals and "bleeding hearts," had simply in the most insidious way trickled out, of history and of ourselves. Remembering those two men now, the one whose very body was the literal reposi- tory of our history, the other who was linked by his uncertain gesture of charity to his friend, I felt terribly diminished, even frightened, because all of my accountings and recountings of those war days, all the furious resolution we all had felt had been as though cellularly obliterated, and it was made clear, as apparently it must be again and again, how limited our moral capacities really are, and, more, that this seems to be a basic fact of human consciousness, the arbitrariness by which our most intense realities are selected to abide or dissipate in the durations we inhabit.

There's something else in looking at the poem again that strikes me as something I hadn't considered as I was writing it; that is, how utterly impassive the narrator is, how much absolutely the observer, how immobile I am there as I watch. I did know as I was working the poem through that I had been in some confusing way a participant in the adventure of the two men, but I realize now that this impassivity was the very substance of my bond with them. There's an element of help- lessness to my regard which seems to correlate exactly to the helplessness of the veteran as he falls and waits to be labored back into his chair. That impassivity and helplessness is, I think, the ironic symbol for me of the actual impotence of those of us who had fought against the war, and then stopped fighting, or stopped understanding what the fight had really been about as our inertias and indolence and personal preoc- cupations overtook us. We were afflicted in a moral sense with as maimed a capacity as the paralytic was in his partial body, and with as confused a notion of necessity as the friend's, whose devotion demands that he reduce himself in dissipation and dissolution.

Much of this, I think, becomes nearly explicit when the friend looks up at me, impales me, it feels like now, with that stare or glare which may or may not be an accusation but which at any rate has intensity enough in it, however inarticulate, to make me look away, to make me cast myself out of the time of the poem into another memory, into a past which is less menacing and less ethically demanding. A remembering which is forgetting. The poem first remembers the friend in his moment of despair or doubt, then looks away again, erasing him utterly, as though to obliterate utterly the demands he might be making of us.

It's that look of his which seems now to me to be the center of the poem, its fulcrum. It's almost as though an experiment had been taking place, and what happens to me, the observer, is that an element in my experiment suddenly makes clear that I am an element in *its*. The impassivity and apparent objectivity, which had seemed at worst mild curiosity, morally neutral, begin to resonate with implications of passivity instead of impassivity, inaction rather than objectivity, and even a withdrawal seems implied, a step back into that other system of omissions and disattentions which seem to be the content of so many of our lost imperatives.

It might be that much of our moral education consists in just such apparently minor, oblique encounters. The human mind seems to have no difficulty in spinning out grand systems of ideals and belief. We doggedly go about grounding ourselves in our metaphysics, in ''greater'' realms, but it is just this sort of confrontation that reveals to us how chancy and contingent those realms actually can be. Faced with someone else's pain, with the raw fact of another's reality, the epiphany always seems to be the same: that the other really does exist in his or her own right, and with exactly the same burning self-awareness that we do. A response is called for from this realization; what that response might be is uncertain, but one thing it has nothing to do with is pity. Pity implies a spiritual attention which might be optional. The urgencies of our encounters consist rather in the potential they have as responsibilities, in demanding of us that we go back into ourselves, to re-form ourselves, to re-situate ourselves in a more self-conscious moral universe.

If there is hope to be found in ''From My Window''—and I think there is—it would be in this. The poem finishes in its look away through time and memory, but perhaps that is because we have to look away before we can begin again. It is so daunting and exhausting to have to confront yet again those questions of accountability which are at the core of our spiritual dialectic. We seem to have to force ourselves again and again to try to reconcile the incongruities of our conscious life, the discrepancies between our intentions and our acts, the astonishing gap between our ability to elaborate admirable ideals and the ease with which we slip from identity to identity to evade them. Whatever hope we do have would seem to have to be found in ourselves, and in our awareness of those others who are the greater moral portion of ourselves.

AUTHOR
BIOGRAPHIES

Stephen Berg has published several books of poems, including *The Daughters, Grief,* and *With Akhmatova at The Black Gates.* He is co-translator, with Diskin Clay, of Sophocles' *Oedipus The King* (O.U.P.), and with Steven Polgar and S. J. Marks, of Miklós Radnóti's *Clouded Sky.* He has received a Guggenheim Fellowship, an NEA Grant, The Frank O'Hara Memorial Prize and is a founding editor of *The American Poetry Review.* Currently he teaches at the Philadelphia College of Art and has completed a new book of poems, *In It,* and *The Ear,* a book of prose pieces. He has edited many other anthologies, including *Naked Poetry* and most recently *In Praise of What Persists.*

Marvin Bell, born 1937 in New York City and raised on eastern Long Island, published his first book, *Things We Dreamt We Died For,* in 1966 with The Stone Wall Press. Thereafter, Atheneum brought out five books of his poems: *A Probable Volume of Dreams,* winner of the Lamont Award in 1969; *The Escape into You,* a book-length sequence, in 1971; *Residue of Song* in 1974; *Stars Which See, Stars Which Do Not See,* a National Book Award finalist, in 1977; and *These Green-Going-to-Yellow* in 1981. A new book, *Drawn by Stones, by Earth, by Things That Have Been in the Fire,* appeared in 1984.

Robert Bly has published numerous books of poetry, including *Silence In The Snowy Fields, The Light Around The Body* and *The Man In The Black Coat Turns.* His essays on poetry, consciousness and community have appeared in various magazines. He has translated the work of many poets: Vallejo, Trakl, Rilke, and Neruda, to name a few. He lives in Moose Lake, Minnesota.

Hayden Carruth has been editor of *Poetry,* poetry editor of *Harper's,* and is an advisory editor for *The Hudson Review.* He has published twenty books, mostly poetry, including *The Sleeping Beauty* and *Brothers, I Loved You All.* His most recent is

319

If You Call This Cry a Song (Countryman Press). For the past three years he has taught at Syracuse University.

James Dickey's books of poetry are *Into The Stone, Drowning With Others, Helmets, Buckdancer's Choice* and *The Eye-Beaters Blood Victory Madness Buckhead and Mercy*. His critical essays include *The Suspect in Poetry* and *Babel to Byzantium*. He has been Consultant in Poetry at the Library of Congress and was awarded the National Book Award. He is also known for his fiction, which includes the novel *Deliverance*.

Stephen Dobyns's fifth book of poems is *Black Dog, Red Dog*. He teaches in the Master of Fine Arts Writing Program of Warren Wilson College, and has written novels and essays. He lives in Watertown, Massachusetts, with his wife and child.

Carolyn Forché was born in Detroit, Michigan, in 1950. Her first book of poems, *Gathering the Tribes*, won the Yale Series of Younger Poets competition in 1976. Her second book of poems, *The Country Between Us*, published by Harper & Row in 1982, received the Lamont Award from the Academy of American Poets. *Flowers from the Volcano* (University of Pittsburgh Press), a translation of the Salvadoran poet, Claribel Alegriá, appeared in 1982. Ms. Forché has held fellowships from the National Endowment for the Arts and the Guggenheim Foundation.

Tess Gallagher's third book of poems, *Willingly*, was published in 1984 by Graywolf Press. Her two previous books are *Instructions to the Double* (1976) and *Under Stars* (1978), both from Graywolf Press. Ms. Gallagher teaches at Syracuse University and spends her summers in Port Angeles, Washington, where she was born. She also writes short stories.

Louise Glück is the author of three collections of poetry: *Firstborn, The House on Marshland,* and *Descending Figure*. She lives with her family in Vermont and teaches at Williams College.

Jorie Graham grew up in Italy and attended the Sorbonne, N.Y.U., Columbia University, and the University of Iowa. She has published two books, *Hybrids of Plants and of Ghosts* (Princeton, 1980) and *Erosion* (Princeton, 1983), and has been the recipient of various awards including an Ingram-Merrill Grant, a Bunting Fellowship, and a Guggenheim Fellowship. She makes her living teaching and is currently living with her husband and child in Iowa City.

Donald Hall lives in New Hampshire, on the family farm, where he supports himself by freelance writing: magazine articles, juveniles, textbooks, plays, memoirs. In 1983 he produced a new play, *Ragged Mountain Elegies*, written in verse and based upon the prose memoir *String too Short to be Saved*. His most recent book of poems is *Kicking the Leaves*, 1978.

Robert Hass lives in Berkeley, California, with his family. His books of poetry include *Praise*, and recently he published a book of essays, *20th Century Pleasures*. Last year he was awarded a MacArthur Fellowship.

Donald Justice was born and brought up in Florida, to which he has recently returned to live. His first book was *The Summer Anniversaries* (1960) and his most recent a volume of selected poems, published by Atheneum in 1979. For it he received the 1980 Pulitzer Prize.

Galway Kinnell's books of poems are *What A Kingdom It Was, Flower Herding on Mount Monadnock, Body Rags, The Book of Nightmares,* and *Mortal Acts Mortal Words*. He has translated the poetry of Francois Villon and Yves Bonnefoy. He was awarded the Pulitzer Prize and now runs the Columbia University Graduate Writing Program and was recently awarded a MacArthur Fellowship.

Etheridge Knight's books of poems are *Belly Song, Poems From Prison,* and *Born of a Woman*. He is currently working on a new collection of poetry to be published by Random House. He has read widely, and currently makes his home in Philadelphia.

Maxine Kumin's most recent collection of poems, *Our Ground Time Here Will Be Brief: New & Selected Poems,* was published by Viking/Penguin in 1982. Viking also published her recent collection of short stories, *Why Can't We Live Together Like Civilized Human Beings?* Kumin, who was Consultant in Poetry to the Library of Congress in 1981–82, won the Pulitzer Prize in 1973 for her poems, *Up Country.* She has taught at Princeton, Brandeis, and Columbia, and served as a Visiting Fellow for the Woodrow Wilson Foundation.

Stanley Kunitz's books over the past fifty-odd years include *Intellectual Things, Passport to the War, Selected Poems 1928–1958,* and *The Testing Tree.* His criticism is collected in *A Kind of Order, A Kind of Folly.* He has won every major award and fellowship, including the Pulitzer Prize, has been an editor of the Yale Younger Poets series, directs the Writing Department of the Fine Arts Work Center in Provincetown, Massachusetts, and has taught in many colleges and universities. He lives in New York City and Provincetown with his wife, the painter Elise Asher. He has read his poetry and lectured in many countries.

Denise Levertov was born in England, has taught at many colleges and universities, and has written both poetry and critical essays. Her books of poetry include *Here and Now, The Jacob's Ladder, The Sorrow Dance, To Stay Alive,* and *Collected Earlier Poems.* She is Fannie Hurst Professor at Brandeis University, and teaches one semester each year at both Stanford and Tufts.

Czeslaw Milosz was born in 1911, in Lithuania. High school and university studies at the University of Wilno, then Poland. During his stay at the university, he was co-founder of a Vanguard literary magazine, which made a name for itself, and one of the leaders of the so-called Second Vanguard in Polish poetry. Received an award for poetry in 1934;

studied in Paris, 1934–35, on a fellowship. During World War II he was active in the Resistance movement in Warsaw as author and editor of clandestine publications. His collected poems, including poems of the Resistance, published in 1945 in Poland, were considered one of the most valid contributions to modern Polish poetry. In a quarrel with "socialist realism," he left Poland in 1951 and until 1960 lived as a freelance writer in France. Awarded Le Prix Littéraire Européen for a novel, 1953. Since 1960 Milosz has lived in Berkeley, California, where he has been Professor of Slavic Languages and Literatures. His output embraces poetry, translations of French, English, and American poetry into Polish (including T. S. Eliot's "The Wasteland"), translations into English, two novels, and literary essays. Recipient of the Neustadt International Prize for Literature, 1978, and the Nobel Prize for Literature, 1980.

"Posthumous Keats" is from **Stanley Plumly's** book *Summer Celestial,* published by Ecco Press. He is currently at work on a collection of essays about contemporary poetry, *Chapter & Verse,* and another volume of poems entitled *Schooling.* He has taught at a number of writing programs around the country, and now teaches in the Creative Writing Program at the University of Houston.

Michael Ryan's essays on poetry have appeared in *American Poetry Review, Antaeus, Poetry,* and *Claims For Poetry,* an anthology of essays by contemporary poets published by the University of Michigan Press. His two books of poetry are *Threats Instead of Trees* (Yale University Press, 1974) and *In Winter* (Holt, Rinehart and Winston, 1981), and he has won numerous awards, including fellowships from the National Endowment for the Arts and the Guggenheim Foundation. He has lived in Italy, traveled in Europe, and recently spent a week in Nicaragua as a guest of the Nicaraguan government. He currently lives in North Garden, Virginia, and is a faculty member of the Warren Wilson College Master of Fine Arts Program for Writers.

Louis Simpson was born in Jamaica. He emigrated to the United States at the age of seventeen, served with the U.S. Army in Europe, then worked in a publishing house and completed his studies at Columbia University. He is the author of ten books of verse, the most recent being *The Best Hour of the Night* (Ticknor & Fields) and *People Live Here: Selected Poems 1949–1983* (BOA Editions). Louis Simpson is also widely known as a literary critic. He lives in Setauket, New York, and teaches at the State University of New York at Stony Brook. His honors and awards include the Pulitzer Prize for poetry and the Medal for Excellence given by Columbia University.

W. D. Snodgrass has published volumes of poetry, criticism, and translations of poetry and of songs and folk ballads. He has taught in several universities and is currently Distinguished Professor of Creative Writing at the University of Delaware. At present, he is working on a volume of new and selected poems. His books of poems include *Hearts Needle*, for which he was awarded a Pulitzer Prize, *After Experience*, and *The Führer Bunker*.

Ted Solotaroff, critic, fiction writer, editor, has published numerous essays on fiction, and edited several books including *Many Windows*, a collection of recent American fiction. He was for many years editor of *The American Review*, and is now Senior Editor for Harper & Row. A book of essays, *The Red-Hot Vacuum*, was published by Godine. Mr. Solotaroff's essay on Kinnell's poem is his first excursion as a critic of poetry.

William Stafford's poems crept out into little magazines from his home in Kansas beginning in the 1940s. In 1960, when he was 46, his first collection appeared, followed in steady succession by six volumes from Harper & Row and a dozen or so volumes from small presses, the latest in each series being *A Glass Face in the Rain* (Harper & Row, 1982) and *Smoke's Way*, selected poems from small presses, 1983, from Graywolf Press.

Gerald Stern is the author of *Rejoicings, Lucky Life, The Red Coal,* and *Paradise Poems.* He teaches at The Writers Workshop, University of Iowa, and spends his summers in Raubsville, Pennsylvania. His column, "Notes from the River," appears regularly in *The American Poetry Review.* "Baja" appears in his book *Paradise Poems.* Recently he spent a semester at the University of Alabama as poet-in-residence.

Lucien Stryk's eleventh book of poems, *Collected Poems 1953–1983,* appeared recently, along with his second spoken album for Folkways Records, *Selected Poems.* He has published a book of essays and interviews with Zenists, *Encounter with Zen: Writings on Poetry and Zen,* has edited *World of the Buddha: An Introduction to Buddhist Literature,* and two anthologies, *Heartland: Poets of the Midwest* (I and II), and translated, with Takashi Ikemoto, a number of collections of Zen poetry, among them, *The Penguin Book of Zen Poetry* (which received the Islands and Continents Translation Award and the Society of Midland Authors Poetry Award), *Zen Poems of China and Japan: The Crane's Bill, On Love and Barley: Haiku of Basho* (a Penguin Classic) and *Triumph of the Sparrow: Zen Poems of Shinkichi Takahashi.* He teaches Oriental literature and poetry at Northern Illinois University.

Robert Penn Warren's novels include *All The King's Men* and *Meet Me in the Green Glen.* He has written many books of poetry: *Brother To Dragons, Selected Poems 1923–75, Now and Then, Or Else, Audubon,* and others. He has also written numerous critical essays on topics as wide ranging as poetry and segregation. He was on the faculty of Yale University for many years, is the recipient of the Pulitzer Prize and several other awards and honorary degrees. He lives in Fairfield, Connecticut, with his wife, the novelist Eleanor Clark.

Theodore Weiss, editor with his wife Renée of the *Quarterly Review of Literature* about to celebrate its 40th anniversary, is a professor of English and Creative Writing at Princeton University. He has published ten books of poetry, most recently a long poem *Recoveries* and *A Short Fuse,* and several books of criticism, the latest of which is *The Man from Porlock*, selected essays, 1944–1981. He was awarded the Brandeis Medal, which he shared with Robert Lowell.

Richard Wilbur went to Amherst, served during World War II with the 36th Infantry Division, became a Junior Fellow at Harvard, and has taught English at Harvard, Wellesley, Wesleyan, and Smith. He has written poems, criticism, children's books, translations, and show lyrics. Recent publications are *Responses* (prose), *Seven Poems, Molière: Four Comedies, Andromache* (translation from Racine), *The Whale* (translations). He is a former president of the American Academy of Arts and Letters.

C. K. Williams has written four books of poems: *Lies, I Am The Bitter Name, With Ignorance,* and *Tar.* He has also published an "hommage" to the poet Issa, *The Lark. The Thrush. The Starling.,* and has written essays on poetry and politics. Mr. Williams is poet-in-residence at George Mason University, lives in Brooklyn and Paris, and was awarded a Guggenheim Fellowship. A new book of poems, each eight lines long, will be published by Random House.